HOW THINGS WORK

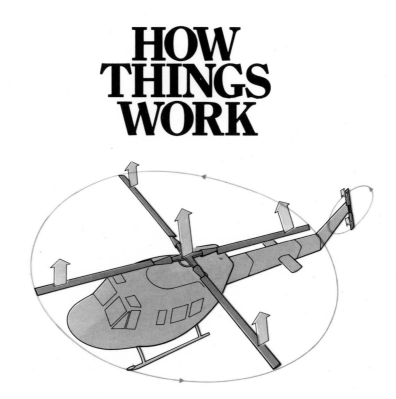

HOW THINGS WORK

Michael Pollard

Larousse and Co. Inc., New York, N.Y.

First published in United States by
Larousse and Co. Inc., 752 5th Avenue,
New York, New York 10036.

Published in Great Britain by
Ward Lock Limited, London, a
member of the Pentos Group.

L.C. Catalog Card number: 78-54638
ISBN 0-88332-097-5

Printed in Hong Kong

Contents

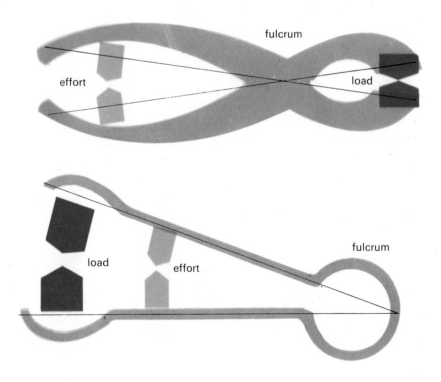

The helicopter

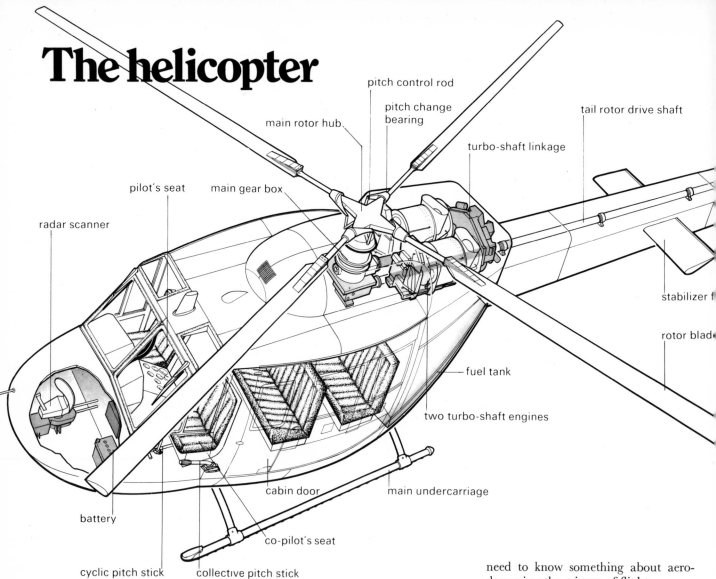

pitch control rod

pitch change bearing

main rotor hub

tail rotor drive shaft

turbo-shaft linkage

pilot's seat

main gear box

radar scanner

stabilizer f

rotor blad

fuel tank

two turbo-shaft engines

cabin door

main undercarriage

battery

co-pilot's seat

cyclic pitch stick

collective pitch stick

Nearly 500 years ago the Italian artist and inventor Leonardo da Vinci drew some designs for a flying-machine that could 'screw itself up in the air'. These were the words he used in his notes under the drawings.

The machine was never built, and in Leonardo's time no one had invented an engine that could have powered it. But what Leonardo had invented was a helicopter. The drawings in his note-books show a machine very much like the helicopters we know today.

It was not until about 1940 that the first working helicopter was built in the United States by Igor Sikorsky. Sikorsky and other designers had added many ideas of their own, but the main principle of Sikorsky's helicopter was the same as Leonardo da Vinci's. On top of the fuselage was a rotor (Leonardo had called it a 'helix', from the Greek word for 'screw') which, as

Leonardo had written, was 'turned with great speed' and enabled the machine 'to screw itself up in the air and rise high'.

If you've ever seen a helicopter at work – perhaps crop-spraying, lifting something into position at the top of a high building, or carrying out a daring rescue at sea – you'll know that it can do much more than merely go up and down. It can fly in any direction – even backwards. It can hover over the same spot. It can make sharper turns than any other kind of aircraft. It needs no runways for landing or taking off. It can do exactly what the pilot wants it to do.

When Igor Sikorsky was showing off his first helicopter, one of his favourite stunts was to lower a bag full of eggs into a circle marked out on the ground – without breaking a single one!

The secret of the helicopter's amazing tricks is in the design of the rotor blades. To understand how these work we

need to know something about aero-dynamics, the science of flight.

When any aircraft flies, there are four different forces at work. The first is the force of gravity, or *weight*, which tends to keep the aircraft (and everything else on Earth) on the ground. To get the air-craft off the ground another force – *lift* – is needed. When you're standing still, your weight keeps your feet on the ground. If you jump up, the muscles in your legs provide the lift that gets you up in the air.

Once an aircraft is airborne, two more forces come into action. One – *drag* – tends to hold the machine back, and the other – *thrust* – is provided by the engine to move the aircraft forward.

A helicopter's rotor blades have to provide both lift and thrust. To do this the blades have to be moved to or 'pitched' at different angles.

If the rotor blades were flat on both sides, they would make a wind as they spun round, but nothing else would happen. In fact, the blades are curved

Left A small passenger-carrying helicopter with room for a pilot, co-pilot and six passengers.
Below right The top diagram shows how the helicopter is lifted by differing air pressure acting on the main rotor blades. The red circle shows the path of the blade tips. The tail rotor revolves vertically, steadying the machine and giving some help in steering. The small diagram shows the different forces which act on a helicopter in flight. At the bottom of the page a typical layout of helicopter controls and instruments. The 'collective pitch' stick moves up and down, controlling the pitch, or tilt, of all the main rotor blades together. The 'cyclic pitch' stick, or 'go-stick', moves backwards and forwards, and varies the pitch of the blades at different points in their cycle. The throttle, working like a motor-cycle throttle, controls the speed of the blades. The tail rotor control is operated by the pilot's feet.

make the helicopter spin about all over the sky, rather like a car in a skid on an icy road. As the blades turned one way, the cabin and fuselage would turn in the opposite direction, and soon the machine would spin out of control. The tail rotor provides just enough power to keep the fuselage in line with the direction the pilot wants to take.

Instead of a tail rotor some large helicopters have two main rotors above the fuselage. These keep the machine steady by revolving in opposite directions. All the blades of both rotors can be pitched together or separately. Because its two rotors give more lift, a twin-rotor

helicopter can carry loads far heavier than the more familiar type.

Igor Sikorsky called his first helicopter 'the pack mule of the air'—and so it has turned out to be. Just as the pack mule can take loads to places that no other kind of land transport can reach, so the helicopter can take off and land in areas too small for other aircraft. It can take troops to clearings in the jungle, take workers and supplies out to oil-rigs in the sea, move in close to a cliff-face to rescue a stranded climber, and hover long enough for surveyors to make accurate measurements of the ground below. Helicopters look clumsy, can't

on top. As they spin, the air rushing over the top takes longer to get past than the air passing underneath. This makes a difference in air pressure, because the air on top has to spread out more thinly to fill the space. So the heavier air pressure underneath lifts the helicopter up.

Unlike the wings of most aircraft the helicopter's rotor blades can be tilted, or 'pitched', at different angles. In this way the pilot can make the air passing over the tops of the blades travel even further, so increasing the lift. Or, once in the air, he can tilt the blades so that the pressures above and below are equal. Then the helicopter will stay at the same height, hovering.

So far the pilot has tilted all the blades at the same angle at the same time, using his 'collective pitch' stick. Now he wants to make the helicopter go forward, and he moves his hand to another control, the 'cyclic pitch' stick. This tilts each blade, as it goes round, at just the right moment to push the helicopter forward, rather like the blade of an oar. As the blade moves on, it tilts back again ready for the next time round. To go backwards or sideways the blades are tilted at different points on their way round.

Most helicopters, like the one in the diagram, have, in addition to the main rotor above the cabin, a second, smaller rotor mounted on the tail. The second rotor's job is to keep the helicopter steady. On its own the main rotor would

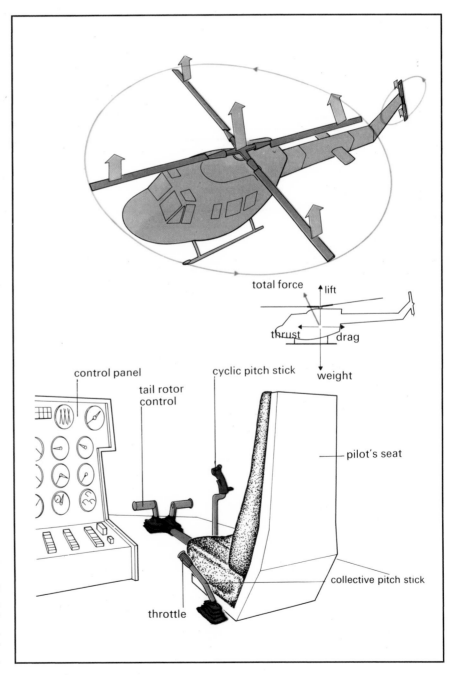

total force — lift
thrust — drag
weight

control panel
tail rotor control
cyclic pitch stick
pilot's seat
collective pitch stick
throttle

travel very fast and make a lot of noise–but they're hard workers.

When Sikorsky developed the helicopter, he hoped that it would become a major means of transport for short journeys. He imagined helicopters making the rounds of a city, picking up people to go to work, rather like buses. Helicopters would also work like taxis, he thought, taking passengers from one place to another and landing on the roofs of high buildings.

Helicopters are used in this way, but nothing like as much as Sikorsky hoped. In Los Angeles many of the taller buildings have landing pads on their roofs. In London a helicopter service connects the city centre with Heathrow Airport. The Queen's husband, Prince Philip, often sets out for duties out of town by boarding (and sometimes piloting) a helicopter in the garden of Buckingham Palace, right in the heart of London. But the use of helicopters in cities has been held back by two things: the possible danger of a crash into crowded city streets, and the noise that helicopters make.

People who want to travel about cities can, after all, always go by road or rail. Where the helicopter really scores is on journeys that can't be made in any other way.

Above Taking supplies to the Arctic by sea involves a long, dangerous voyage that can be made only in summer. For ordinary aircraft it means tricky landings on icy runways. The helicopter–here delivering a supply of timber to a remote scientific station–provides the answer.

Left For the very rich 'fun helicopters' are an interesting hobby. In large, open areas of the world like the Midwest of the United States and some parts of Africa and Australia one-man helicopters like this Bensen enable farmers and landowners to cover a lot of ground in a short time. But for most of us a helicopter in the garage alongside the car remains a dream–or a nightmare.

Opposite Armies all over the world find helicopters useful. They can work in city streets or jungles, ferrying troops to trouble-spots, evacuating wounded soldiers or searching for terrorists. The all-Perspex cabins of these Bell 'Sioux' machines make them especially suitable for search and observation duties, giving the crew an 'all-round' view.

The airship

People who have travelled in an airship say that it's the nicest way to fly. Airships fly lower than aeroplanes, so passengers have a marvellous view of the countryside. The flight is smooth and quiet, and passengers have plenty of room to move about.

There have been no regular passenger flights by airship for over forty years, but in the 1930s they provided the first transatlantic air service between Europe and America. But the service was stopped after the airship *Hindenburg* caught fire and crashed as it came into Lakehurst Field in New Jersey in the United States of America.

Since then, airships have been used by the United States Navy–the sailors call them 'blimps'–and for advertising, but not for regular services. Some people believe, though, that they could be useful as cargo-carriers.

Airships are really balloons with engines–and that was just what the first ones looked like. The very first, powered by a steam-engine, flew in 1852 in France. But it gave a very bumpy ride

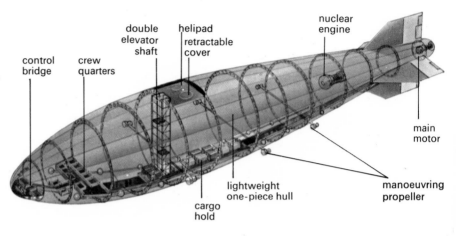

control bridge — crew quarters — double elevator shaft — helipad retractable cover — nuclear engine — main motor — manoeuvring propeller — lightweight one-piece hull — cargo hold

and was almost impossible to steer.

Like many other modern inventions the airship was designed for use in war. The most famous airship-builder was a German soldier, Count von Zeppelin, whose first airship flew in 1900. He gave it, instead of a flexible balloon, a rigid outer skin built on a framework of girders. This enabled him to build it much larger, so that it would not be buffeted about by the wind. By this time

the internal combustion engine had been invented, and he used this instead of steam-power.

Zeppelin's first airship was huge–128 metres long. He went on to build a fleet of 100 airships for the German forces. After World War 1 Germany, Britain and the United States all built airships for passenger services.

The really amazing thing about airships is their size. The 'body', containing the gas that keeps the airship aloft, has to be enormous to give the machine enough 'lift'. But once at their cruising height, airships can be driven along by quite small engines. This is because the cigar-shaped 'body' offers little resistance to wind pressure, while the whole airship is held up by the gas. The engines of an aeroplane have to give enough power to keep it up in the air as well as drive it along.

The gas in an airship is lighter than air. A lot of gas is needed, and so airship-builders had to use a gas that was cheap. They chose hydrogen–and this was where the trouble started. Hydrogen catches fire easily. Almost all the disasters that happened to airships were caused by the explosion of their hydrogen.

Present-day airships use helium, a gas which does not catch fire. This means that airships are now safe.

No one can say whether the airship will make a come-back–but there are many people who would like it to do so, especially for cargo. Perhaps, in your lifetime, the great and graceful airship will once again glide almost silently across the sky.

Above A designer's idea for the airship of the future. The crew's quarters and the cargo hold are in the body instead of in 'gondolas' hanging underneath as in most airships built so far. Craft like this could carry cargo which is too heavy or bulky to go by aeroplane.
Left Huge sheds are needed for the building and storage of airships. This was part of the Zeppelin factory in Germany in the 1930s. The tiny figures of workers on the floor show the size of the place.
Opposite The Goodyear Tyre Company has been building airships since 1924. This one, *Europa,* is used to advertise the company's name and is often seen at air shows and displays. But it is also a reminder that the airship, forgotten by so many people, could still have a future in the world of transport.

The parachute

When men began to fly, it wasn't long before they needed a way of escaping from an aircraft in trouble.

They found the answer in an idea first thought up nearly 500 years ago by the Italian artist and designer Leonardo da Vinci. It was the parachute.

In Leonardo's time there was no use for the parachute because there were no aircraft to fall from. But in 1797, over 100 years before the first aeroplane flight, a Frenchman named Garnerin made the first parachute drop from a balloon. Leonardo's idea, Garnerin's parachute and the parachutes used today all look similar, but today's are made of nylon, a man-made fabric invented in the last fifty years.

Parachutes are easy to understand. The umbrella-shaped top is called the canopy. When this opens out, the air trapped inside the umbrella resists the weight of the falling parachutist and so slows him up. There is a small hole in the top of the canopy which allows some air to stream through from underneath. Without this the parachute would drop too slowly and drift sideways in the wind.

Suspension lines lead from the outside

Above right An Apollo capsule, returning to Earth after a space flight, travels the last few hundred metres by parachute. US spacecraft 'splash down' in the ocean, but it is believed that some Russian craft parachute to solid ground.
Below High-speed aircraft on landing must reduce speed quickly if they are to stop before reaching the end of the runway. This Short SC1 aircraft is using a parachute, which opens on landing, to slow it down. Just as in an ordinary parachute, air collected in the canopy provides resistance.

edge of the canopy to a harness strapped on the parachutist's back.

Before a parachutist takes off for a jump, his harness and the pack into which the parachute is folded are checked carefully. Everything must work perfectly first time, because in parachuting there are no second chances! The parachute canopy and lines are all folded into the pack so that when the time comes everything will come out in the right order, with no snagging or twisting.

When it's time for the parachutist to jump, he lets himself fall clear of the aircraft before he opens his 'chute. If he didn't, it might get caught in the slipstream – the air currents round the aircraft. Once clear, he pulls the rip-cord on the pack, and it opens. A small parachute, called the 'pilot parachute'

or 'drogue', comes out first. The air opens this out, and as it opens it pulls out the main canopy and suspension lines. When the canopy is open and the suspension lines have pulled tight underneath, the parachutist feels a jerk and he begins to float in the air instead of falling. Then he knows that he's safe – for the moment, at least.

Modern parachutes have slots in the canopy, and by pulling on the lines these can be altered in shape. In this way the parachutist can steer towards a spot that looks safe for landing

The landing is the trickiest part of a parachute jump. If possible, the parachutist steers towards the softest-looking spot he can see. As he lands, he relaxes so that the shock of hitting the ground doesn't jar his legs or spine, and then he rolls over to break the fall. As soon as he can, he pulls a trigger on his harness to free himself from the parachute, so that it doesn't drag him along. The parachutist's first job on landing is to gather up his parachute so that it can be inspected, repacked and used again.

Some parachutes are designed to open automatically without anyone pulling a rip-cord. If the pilot of a modern fighter aircraft has to bale out, he presses a button in the cockpit which operates an ejector seat. This shoots him, seat and all, upwards, clear of the aircraft, before he begins to drop. Then his parachute opens by itself. The ejector seat enables the pilot to escape quickly without the difficulty of climbing out of the cockpit of a fast-moving aircraft.

Automatic parachutes are used, too, by space capsules in their return to Earth. When the returning capsule is a few hundred metres from the target area where it is to land, its parachutes automatically open to make a soft landing.

Parachutes are not used in airliners, partly because they fly too high for parachutes to be of any use, but mainly because the use of a parachute involves plenty of practice and training. Soldiers trained for parachute-jumping are often used in areas—such as jungle clearings—which cannot be reached by road and in areas behind the enemy's lines. Guns, armoured cars and supplies are also dropped by parachute. Food and clothing are sometimes dropped to people cut off by floods or snow.

Some people go parachuting for fun. 'Free fall' parachutists, sometimes called sky-divers, fall about 2,500 metres before opening their parachutes, often doing aerobatics, either separately or together, on the way down.

Above By pulling on the suspension lines this parachutist can change the shape of the slots in the canopy and so steer himself by swinging from side to side. The pilot parachute, or 'drogue', can be seen at the bottom right of the main canopy.

Left Two stages in a 'free fall' parachute drop. 'Free fall' parachutists start their falls at a height of about 3,000 metres and open their parachutes when they are about 600 metres from the ground.

Sky-divers falling in a 'ten-man star' formation.

The jet engine

If you blow up a balloon and let it go without tying the end, it will zoom around until all the air inside it is exhausted. The thrust of the air inside, struggling to get out, pushes the balloon forward.

This is the principle put to work in a jet engine. Huge quantities of air are sucked in at the front of the engine and put under pressure, like the air in the balloon. Fuel is sprayed into the compressed air to make a mixture which burns fiercely. The hot gases which rush to escape from the engine's tailpipe provide the thrust to drive the aircraft forward.

Jet engines are used nowadays instead of piston engines for almost all but the smallest aircraft. For their weight jets are more powerful. They have fewer working parts and so can be maintained more cheaply. The fuel they use is kerosene, which is cheaper than the petrol used in piston engines and less likely to catch fire.

The thrust of a jet's exhaust gases can be used directly to push the aircraft forward, and this is what happens in the ramjet type of engine. But in most engines the hot gases are used first to drive a turbine, and this provides the power to suck in and compress more air at the front.

The first jet engines, built in the 1930s, worked in this way. They were turbojets, like the engine in the top diagram on this page.

Since the first jets were made, there have been many improvements and new ideas to give them even more power.

In the turboprop engine the turbine is connected both with the compressor and with a set of propeller blades mounted at the front. An aircraft fitted with turboprops is pushed through the air by the exhaust gases *and* pulled by the propellers that those gases have helped to turn.

Turbofan engines, sometimes called fanjets, take the turboprop idea a stage further. In the turbofan the propeller blades—many more than in an ordinary propeller—are enclosed in the body of the engine. As they make more efficient use of their fuel, turbofans are less expensive to run than other types of jet engine. And because all the working

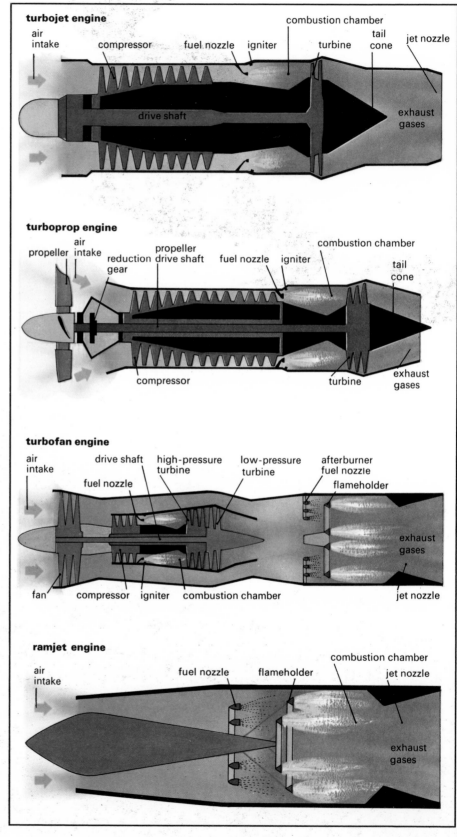

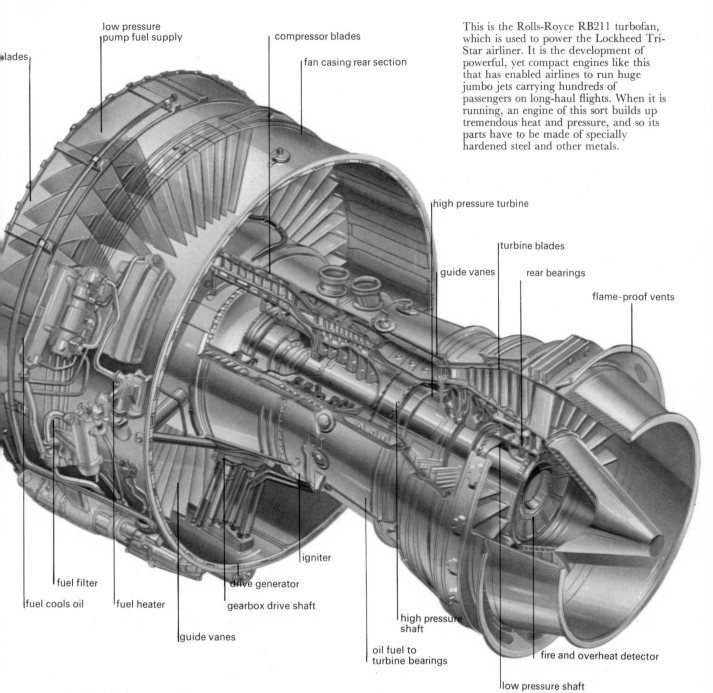

low pressure
pump fuel supply

blades

compressor blades

fan casing rear section

This is the Rolls-Royce RB211 turbofan, which is used to power the Lockheed Tri-Star airliner. It is the development of powerful, yet compact engines like this that has enabled airlines to run huge jumbo jets carrying hundreds of passengers on long-haul flights. When it is running, an engine of this sort builds up tremendous heat and pressure, and so its parts have to be made of specially hardened steel and other metals.

high pressure turbine

turbine blades

guide vanes

rear bearings

flame-proof vents

igniter

fuel filter

fuel cools oil

fuel heater

drive generator

gearbox drive shaft

guide vanes

high pressure shaft

oil fuel to turbine bearings

fire and overheat detector

low pressure shaft

parts are enclosed, they are quieter.

The turbofan in the diagram is fitted with afterburners which heat up the exhaust gases and give them an extra thrust as they escape. Afterburners are sometimes also fitted to turbojets to give them extra power. The turbojets in the French Mirage and Russian MiG-21 fighters, and in the Concorde airliner have afterburners.

The ramjet is a special kind of engine which can only work when the aircraft or missile to which it is fitted is already travelling very fast. It has no compressor or turbine. Air is forced in by the speed of the aircraft and compressed by the shape of the engine. Then it is burned in a mixture with fuel and forced out again. With no compressor it cannot produce enough thrust to power an aircraft from the start of its flight, but it can be used to give extra power to an aircraft also fitted with turbojets or turbofans. The ramjet is also used in missiles to 'take over' power once they have been fired by rocket.

We usually think of jets as aircraft engines, but they are used in other ways as well. Hovercraft use jets to provide the cushion of air that enables them to glide over the water. Jets are too powerful to be used in ordinary cars, but in the United States an experimental jet-powered car has travelled at more than 1,000 kph. Turbofan engines have also been used to pump natural gas through pipeline networks, and in electricity power stations.

As anyone knows who lives near an airport, one of the great problems posed by jet engines is noise. The jets of the future will probably be similar to those in use today—but they will be quieter.

Supersonic flight

We live in the supersonic age. For the first time in history people can travel faster than sound. A supersonic airliner could whisk you across the Atlantic in three and a half hours, or take only nine hours to fly you from Europe to the Far East.

But why is the speed of sound so important to travel by air? What's the connection between sound and flying?

Until about thirty years ago it was thought that flying faster than sound would be impossible. Scientists talked of the 'sound barrier'. If an aircraft flew faster than sound, some of them thought, it would hit the 'sound barrier' and fall to pieces. Then, one day in 1947 an American test pilot proved them wrong. He flew his rocket-powered Bell X-1 experimental plane above the speed of sound – and landed safely. And, what was more, the pilot himself was quite fit. Doctors had feared that the human brain might not be able to stand up to supersonic flight. With these worries over, the story of supersonic flight could begin.

Later, other test pilots and jet-fighter pilots broke the 'sound barrier'. They came to no harm – but as they approached the speed of sound, and flew even faster, strange things happened.

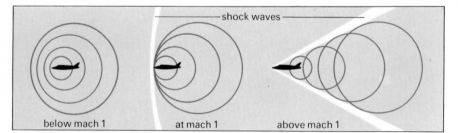

shock waves

below mach 1   at mach 1   above mach 1

Their aircraft began to shake violently. The controls went 'dead' – the pilots couldn't steer. And the strangest thing of all was reported by people on the ground. As the aircraft went over, flying faster than sound, there was a sharp crack like thunder. As the aircraft flashed across the sky, this noise followed on the ground below.

The speed of sound at sea level is about 1,200 kph. High in the air, sound travels more slowly. But at whatever speed it is travelling the speed of sound is called 'Mach 1'.

When an aircraft is flying slower than Mach 1, the sound of its engines travels along with it. You hear it coming, you see it overhead, and then you hear it fade away into the distance. The sound-waves travel from the engines to your ears, disturbing the air slightly as they go.

If the aircraft speeds up towards Mach 1, the pattern of the sound-waves round it changes. The waves trail out behind, and at the same time a pressure wave, or 'shock wave', builds up in front. This is the 'sound barrier'. You can't see it, but it's there just the same. To fight against this shock wave the aircraft has to put on more power, and this is why supersonic aircraft use very much more fuel than any others. Pushing against the shock wave with tremendous power, the aircraft has to put up with huge stresses and strains. For this reason scientists once feared that it would shake itself to bits trying to break the 'sound barrier'.

Aircraft designed to fly supersonically must be able to stand the shock wave that builds up at Mach 1. Going faster than Mach 1, there are more problems. The shock wave makes a V-shape in front of the nose and tries to pull the nose

Right Another supersonic warplane is the North American A-5 Vigilante bomber.

Left The delta-winged XB-70 Valkyrie has flown at Mach 3 – three times the speed of sound. As in the Anglo-French Concorde the delta-wing shape enables the XB-70 to stand up to the huge shock waves of high-speed flight.

downwards. If this were to happen, the plane would go into a dive. At the same time the air rushing past the fuselage makes it very hot – hot enough to melt some metals. And on top of all that the wings have to meet fierce pressure as they cut through the air.

One way of solving the nose-dropping problem is used in the Anglo-French Concorde, the first passenger aircraft to fly supersonically. As Concorde approaches Mach 1, the fuel stored in its wings is pumped from the front tanks to the back, giving more weight at the back and so lifting the nose. This is rather like putting more weights on one pan of a set of scales in order to keep the balance level.

The heat problem is solved by using alloys – mixtures of metal – which contain titanium. Titanium is a 'miracle metal' which melts only at very high temperatures.

As for the wings, tests have shown that delta-shaped wings, like those of a paper dart, are best for standing up to the pressures of supersonic flight. Concorde has wings of this shape. Some other supersonic planes have 'swing-wings'. Below the speed of sound their wings stick out to the sides in the usual way. As Mach 1 is reached, the wings swing back to make a delta-shape.

Although aircraft designers have been able to solve the problems of aircraft flying through the 'sound barrier', they have not been able to do much about the complaints of people on the ground. The shock wave that makes a 'sonic boom' as an aircraft passes Mach 1 can also break windows and even damage buildings, especially old ones.

There is no way of avoiding the noise and possible damage when aircraft fly supersonically over land. Possibly people wouldn't mind the sonic boom so much if they had warning of it. But when an aircraft is flying faster than sound, all its sound trails out behind the pressure wave it has set up. So you hear the sonic boom first and the sound of the engine afterwards. If you have ever been under the flight path of a supersonic aircraft, you will know what a shock this can give you! But the problem of damage to property is even worse. It is impossible to prove that damage was done by one particular aircraft, and in any case the damage may show itself only much later.

For all these reasons Concorde reaches supersonic speeds only when it is over the sea, and pilots of supersonic military aircraft have strict instructions not to fly faster than sound over towns and cities. Some countries have even refused to allow supersonic aircraft anywhere near them. Flying faster than sound is fine if you are a passenger. If you're living on the ground below, it can be a noisy nuisance.

Left The diagrams show the changing pattern of sound- and shock waves as an aircraft approaches and passes Mach 1.
Right Noise is one of the major problems posed by supersonic flight. An aircraft flying over land at Mach 1 or above creates a cone-shaped 'noise corridor', shown in blue in the diagram. The red area shows the 'sonic boom' zone where the noise cone meets the ground. People in the red area will hear a sonic boom, and damage may be caused to glasshouses and old buildings. As the aircraft flies on, the 'sonic boom' zone will cut a path across the countryside. Flights by supersonic passenger aircraft are planned so that speeds above Mach 1 are reached only over the sea or uninhabited land areas.

noise cone

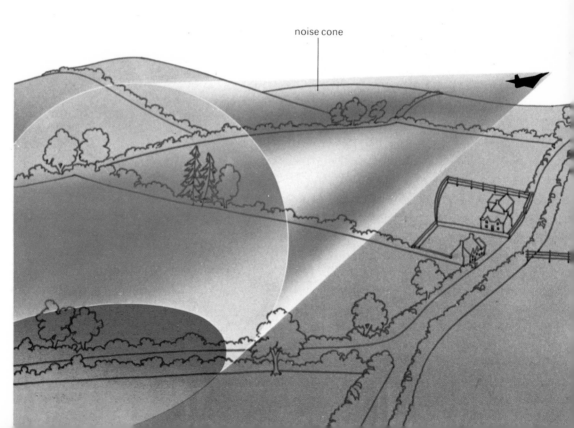

Radar

Radar is one of the many inventions that began as a means of defence in wartime and has now been put to many peaceful uses. In fact, modern sea and air travel – and even weather forecasting – would not be possible without it.

If you stand in an open space and shout loudly, you will hear an echo bounce back from the buildings round about. If you could measure accurately the time it takes for your voice to travel to the buildings and back again, you could work out how far away they are. This is how radar works, but it makes use of radio- rather than sound-waves.

The two main parts of a radar set are the antennae, or aerials, usually dish-shaped, and the screen in front of the radar operator. The aerials send out a beam of strong radio-waves. Any object in the path of the beam 'catches' some of the waves and echoes them back to the aerials, which pick them up. The echoes

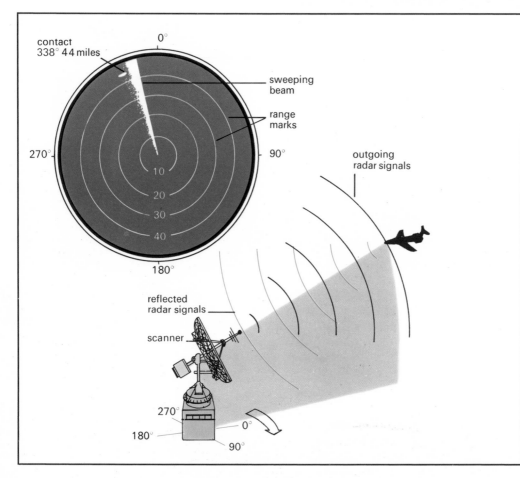

Above The curved antenna, or 'scanner', of an airfield radar, and *(left)* how it works. The circular track of the antenna is shown on the circular radar screen with marks to show distances from the radar. As the antenna moves round, its track is shown by the beam of light, or 'sweep', and as it revolves it picks up echoes from objects in its path. The antenna of this radar has picked up echoes from the approaching aircraft. These show as a 'blip' to the left of the sweep on the screen.
Below Nature's radar, the bat. Bats are almost blind, but they avoid obstacles by sending out high-pitched squeaks which are bounced back like radar signals.

from near objects return sooner than those from objects further away. The returning radio-waves are shown up as a series of 'blips', or points of light, on the screen.

The aerials cannot transmit waves and receive them at the same time, so they do each job in turn. Waves are sent out for a fraction of a second–called a pulse–and then there is a pause for another fraction of a second while the aerials receive any returning waves. In most radar systems the antennae are mounted in a dish-shaped 'scanner' which can be moved to point in the direction the operator chooses. An airfield radar operator will want to know about *all* the aircraft in the area of the airfield, and his radar scanner will revolve all the way round, bringing in signals from every point of the compass. An operator working at the end of one particular runway, however, will want to know only about those aircraft approaching that runway. His scanner will swing to and fro to cover just that sector of the sky.

Objects show up on the screen in different strengths and sizes. On an airfield radar a large airliner would show up more clearly than a small private plane. Objects made of metal show up more clearly than others because they bounce radio-waves back more strongly. The radar operator watches his screen and can tell which object is which by the size of the 'blips' and the speed at which they are moving.

Aircraft themselves also carry radar equipment. It helps the crew to navigate and also shows up other aircraft that may be moving along the same stretch of busy airway. Military aircraft use radar to find their targets and to show up enemy planes or missiles.

Military radar can be used for defence as well as attack. Many countries have set up chains of very powerful scanners near their borders, facing the direction from which an enemy attack would be most likely to come. These scanners, searching the sky non-stop day and night, can pick up signals from enemy aircraft or missiles and relay details instantly to fighter stations or anti-missile defence crews.

Radar is used in many other ways besides controlling the movement of aircraft. Busy stretches of water such as the English Channel and the St Lawrence Seaway are also watched by radar so that collisions can be avoided.

By watching a screen on the bridge of his ship a ship's master can navigate more accurately than by using his eyes, especially when visibility is poor. The disturbed air in storms and hurricanes sends back a strong radar echo, and weather forecasters can spot bad weather this way. Radar is even used to control speed on the roads. Radar sets on the roadside measure the speed of passing vehicles and help the police to pick out those which are going too fast.

Top In the area round a large airport at any one time there may be a large number of aircraft about to land or take off. A close watch on air traffic is vital to safety. This controller has in addition to the two screens in front of him the large screen to his right which shows the tracks of all the aircraft currently in the area.

Above Radar systems scan the skies to give warning of enemy aircraft or missile attacks. This is a fixed system of aerials set up to send out signals in the direction from which an enemy attack might be expected to come.

Rockets

At a fireworks display watchers clap and cheer as fireworks shoot up into the sky, exploding into balls of coloured light. . .

On duty in his watch-tower a coast-guard sees a light in the sky out at sea. A red flare! He reaches for the emergency phone. . . .

At the space centre a man's voice comes over the loudspeakers. Five . . . four . . . three . . . two . . . one . . . ignition . . . lift-off! We have lift-off!

The fireworks, the ship's distress signal and the space flight are just three of the ways in which rockets are used.

When you light the touch paper of a firework rocket, the heat sets light to gunpowder inside the tube. The gunpowder burns fiercely, sending out streams of hot gas. There's not enough room for all the gas inside the rocket, so it rushes out through the open bottom of the tube. The rush of gas pushes the rocket upwards – and it carries on until the gunpowder has burned out and the gas is exhausted. Then the empty rocket falls back to earth.

A space rocket works in a similar way – but with one very important difference. Once a gunpowder rocket

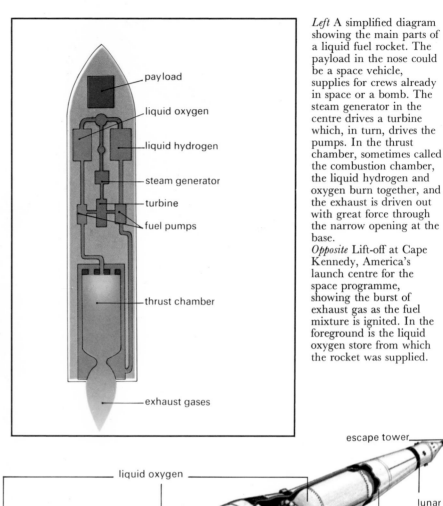

payload
liquid oxygen
liquid hydrogen
steam generator
turbine
fuel pumps
thrust chamber
exhaust gases

Left A simplified diagram showing the main parts of a liquid fuel rocket. The payload in the nose could be a space vehicle, supplies for crews already in space or a bomb. The steam generator in the centre drives a turbine which, in turn, drives the pumps. In the thrust chamber, sometimes called the combustion chamber, the liquid hydrogen and oxygen burn together, and the exhaust is driven out with great force through the narrow opening at the base.

Opposite Lift-off at Cape Kennedy, America's launch centre for the space programme, showing the burst of exhaust gas as the fuel mixture is ignited. In the foreground is the liquid oxygen store from which the rocket was supplied.

escape tower

lunar pac

guidance system

liquid oxygen

liquid hydrogen

J-2 engine

hydrocarbon fuel

liquid hydrogen

J-2 engines

F-1 engines

The Saturn V multi-stage rocket which was used for the first moon landing by US astronauts Neil Armstrong and 'Buzz' Aldrin in 1969. The hydrocarbon fuel used in the first stage was kerosene. The whole launcher was 85 metres high.

is lit, it will go on burning until all the fuel runs out. There is no way of controlling it. And you can't switch the rocket off for a while and switch it on again later on in its journey. Space rockets use liquid fuel, which is stored in tanks and pumped to the combustion chamber in the base of the rocket where it is burned. If necessary, the pumps can be slowed down or stopped altogether, and in this way the speed of the rocket engine is controlled.

Many different kinds of liquid fuel have been tried in rockets, but liquid oxygen, liquid hydrogen and kerosene are the fuels most often used. Kerosene is safe, but large quantities of it are needed to provide the thrust that a rocket needs for lift-off. This takes up valuable space and adds to the rocket's weight. Liquid hydrogen and liquid oxygen are lighter and take up less room.

Oxygen and hydrogen at normal Earth temperatures are both gases. They are turned into liquids by being cooled. This also compresses them into a smaller space, in much the same way as liquid water takes up less space than ice.

When the rocket is ready to be launched, the fuel–liquid hydrogen or kerosene–is mixed with liquid oxygen in the combustion chamber. This is rather like the boiler of a central-heating system, made with immensely strong material to withstand the heat and pressure of the burning fuel. When the mixture is lit, the only way for the hot gases to get out of the combustion chamber is through the hole at the base. As the heat and thrust build up, the rocket lifts off the launching pad–and another space journey has begun.

The hardest work a rocket has to do is to push itself away from the Earth and out of the Earth's atmosphere. One rocket couldn't do this on its own. So the huge rockets that launch spacecraft, like the Saturn V rocket used for the Apollo moon landings, are really several rockets joined together. These are called 'multi-stage' rockets. Each stage takes the spacecraft part of the way, and then the next stage carries on.

This is how a multi-stage moon launch works. The first stage–nearest the ground–is the most powerful one, and its job is to drive the craft upwards out of the Earth's atmosphere. In the Saturn V this stage has a rocket fuelled by kerosene and liquid oxygen. When the fuel of the first stage runs out, the stage drops away and is burned up as it

re-enters the atmosphere. Meanwhile, the second stage starts to work, pushing the spacecraft on until it goes into Earth orbit. By this time it is already travelling at 29,000 kph. Once in orbit, it will stay there without using its engines, and because it is going so fast it needs only a small 'kick' to push it out of orbit and on its way to the moon. The work of the second stage is now over, and it separates. The third stage provides the thrust to take the spacecraft onwards.

As well as the three main rocket stages the moon exploration vehicles also have smaller rockets of their own. Once in space, where there are no forces like gravity or friction to hold a moving object back, only small amounts of thrust are needed to power a space vehicle. These smaller rockets are used to steer the space vehicle into position for the moon landing, to lift it off from the moon's surface and to return the spacemen to orbit and eventually to Earth.

In space flights rockets are even used instead of brakes! A rocket thrusts itself away from the stream of hot gas that it sends out. So if a rocket is fired in the same direction as a spacecraft is already moving, it will push against the direction of travel and slow the craft down. Rockets designed to do this are called 'retro-rockets'. Spacemen use them to slow down their craft ready to re-enter the Earth's atmosphere.

The first liquid fuel rocket, using liquid oxygen and petrol, was launched by an American, Robert Goddard, in 1926. It was about one metre high and it flew for $2\frac{1}{2}$ seconds, reaching a height of about sixty metres. Goddard had already talked of sending a rocket to the moon. 'We'll believe it when we see it!' scoffed the *New York Times*. Goddard didn't live to see it – he died in 1945 – but the *New York Times* did.

It was on 16 July 1969 that three Americans – Neil Armstrong, Edwin 'Buzz' Aldrin and Michael Collins set out from Cape Kennedy on the rocket flight that would make two of them – Armstrong and Aldrin – the first men on the moon.

Left Another United States rocket, the Thor. Like the first stage of the Saturn V this used a kerosene and liquid oxygen mixture. Thor rockets were used to put many US research satellites into orbit, including the first weather satellite to aid forecasting by reporting weather conditions on Earth from orbit.

Space exploration

There are only about fifty people in the world – including one woman – who really know what it's like in space. They are nearly all Americans or Russians. Most of them have spent their time in space flying in orbit round the Earth. A few have been as far as the moon.

Man has always wanted to explore space, just as he has always wanted to fly. But it is only in the past twenty years or so that he has been able to venture outside the Earth's atmosphere.

There are two main problems about space travel. The first is how to get there. The second is how, once there, man can stay alive.

Everything on the Earth and in the Earth's atmosphere is kept there by the force of gravity. If it were not for gravity, everything would go spinning off into space as the Earth turned. To go into space a spacecraft has to break out of the Earth's gravity. It takes a huge amount of energy to do this, and it is only recently that rockets powerful enough have been invented. In the articles on *Rockets* (page 22) and *Satellites* (page 30) you can read how it is done.

But in a space mission men are as important as the craft in which they travel. Man is designed for living on Earth. The air in Earth's atmosphere contains oxygen, which he must breath to stay alive. Man is used to living in Earth temperatures. He eats and drinks things that are grown or made on Earth.

The Earth's atmosphere, as well as giving him air to breath, protects him from many harmful rays that exist in space.

In space there is no oxygen. There is no food or water. It is sometimes much colder and sometimes much hotter than on Earth. There is no protection from harmful radiation. Without special clothing and equipment and a carefully built spacecraft man would undoubtedly die.

There is another problem. In order to break through the 'pull' of gravity space rockets are blasted off at tremendous speeds. The shock of the blast-off would kill a spaceman if he did not wear a special suit.

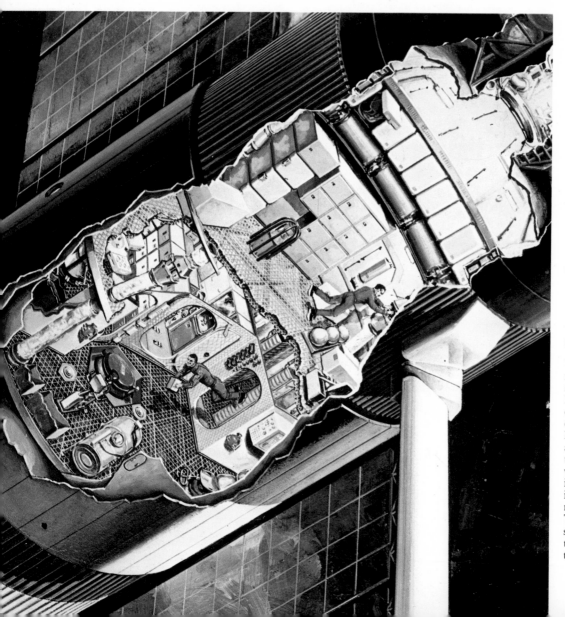

Left Inside Skylab, the US orbiting space laboratory which was launched on 1 May 1973. Three different crews visited Skylab while it was in use, and one crew lived in it for eighty-five days. This crew came back to Earth in February 1974. Skylab was so well-equipped that the crews were able to lead near-normal lives, including taking a daily shower. One aim of the mission was to find out if men could live safely in space for long periods. When doctors checked the health of the returning crews, they found that the long stay in space had done them no harm.

Opposite This spacesuit, with its own built-in 'life support' system, was used by the astronauts on the US Apollo missions to the moon. It is really two suits – a pressurized inner layer and a glass-fibre outer suit which was designed to reflect the heat of the sun. The astronaut's breathing, temperature and heartbeat were checked by instruments which radioed information back to mission control on Earth. The moonshoes were specially weighted because there is little gravity on the moon.

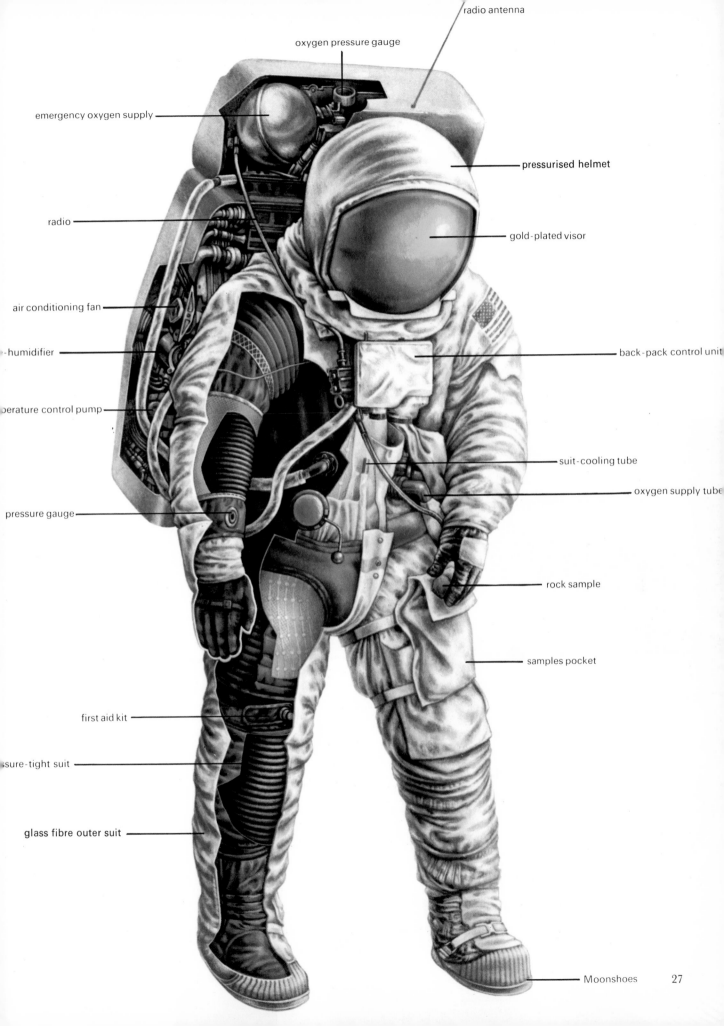

radio antenna

oxygen pressure gauge

emergency oxygen supply

pressurised helmet

gold-plated visor

radio

air conditioning fan

-humidifier

back-pack control unit

erature control pump

suit-cooling tube

oxygen supply tube

pressure gauge

rock sample

samples pocket

first aid kit

sure-tight suit

glass fibre outer suit

Moonshoes 27

So spacemen have to take with them everything they need to keep them alive—food, drink, air, warmth and protection, both from the shock of the launch and from radiation. As there is no air pressure in space, they have to take their own air pressure as well—either inside the cabin or inside their own spacesuits.

Before the first man went into space, unmanned spacecraft were sent up. These had instruments and cameras so that they could report back by radio on what conditions were like. Would the sun's rays burn up the spacecraft? How hot or cold was it? Would it be possible to talk by radio from a spacecraft to Earth? How well would a man be able to see in space? These were some of the questions that the unmanned missions had to answer. All this information helped scientists to design suits and craft that would be safe and suitable for man to use.

One of the strange things about space is that because there is no gravity everything is weightless. This means that a man moving about in a spacecraft floats in the air unless he can manage to hold on to something. If he wants to go to sleep, he has to strap himself down. If he didn't he would float up to the ceiling. If he drops something, it floats about instead of falling to the floor. Many ordinary tools that we use on Earth are no good for space work. It would be no good trying to use your weight to undo a bolt with a spanner, for example. It would be *you* that turned instead of the bolt!

This means that when spacemen train for their missions they have to learn new rules about moving in weightless space. Just as a baby finds everything in the world strange and has to learn how to move about, so spacemen have to start learning all over again. Nothing that they know about moving on Earth will be of any use to them in space.

Some spacecraft, like the American Skylab space laboratory which was sent up in 1973, are so big that their crews can move about in them quite freely without heavy spacesuits and helmets. To overcome the problems of weightlessness the Skylab crew were provided with handrails and special shoes which locked into the floor. But in other ways they lived quite normal lives, eating ordinary food and working on experiments in much the same way as they would have done on Earth.

But if any of the crew wanted to go outside—perhaps to repair some of the equipment or to make tests—he had to put on a special spacesuit. Inside a spacesuit a man is completely cut off from the world around him. He carries his air supply on his back, and has a heater and air-conditioner to keep him comfortable. He can speak only by radio. The suit is pressurized so that he is living in the same pressure as if he were still on Earth.

The most exciting space flights so far have been the Apollo moon landings. The first was on 20 July 1969. Millions of people all over the world, watching their television screens, held their breath as the American lunar module, with astronauts Neil Armstrong and 'Buzz' Aldrin on board, landed on the moon's surface. A few moments later they saw the module's hatchway open and Neil Armstrong climb down a ladder to become the first-ever man on the moon.

Neil Armstrong and 'Buzz' Aldrin could stay on the moon for only just over two hours, but later Apollo moon missions stayed longer. They even took with them a little car, the 'moon rover', which meant that they could explore further away from the landing-place.

Future space flights will take man even further into space. Already unmanned missions to Mars and Venus have prepared the way for manned flights. Every successful mission gives us the knowledge—and the ambition—to venture further.

Left The 'moon rover' at work during one of the Apollo moon missions. Like the astronaut's moonshoes the car was made especially heavy so that it would stay on the moon's surface. It was used to carry instruments for measuring temperature, pressure and radiation as well as to carry the astronauts about.

Above 'Buzz' Aldrin, one of the first two men on the moon, using an instrument to measure moonquake shocks. In the background is the lunar module that Armstrong and Aldrin used to reach the moon from the command module.
Right Another view of the 'moon rover'. Its tyres were similar to the tyres used on Earth, but because the moon has no air pressure to push against the tyre walls only a little air was needed inside them.

Satellites

Wherever the Earth travels in space, the moon goes too. Earth and moon together travel round the sun, taking a year to go all the way round. At the same time the moon moves round the Earth, making the complete trip once every 29½ days. The moon is a satellite of the Earth and moves round it in orbit.

Some other planets have several moons as satellites. We have only one. But we also have a number of artificial satellites—objects moving in orbit round the Earth that man has put there.

Below Two Russian satellites on show. The 10-tonne Proton 1, in the background, has large solar batteries in the four fins. These collect energy from the sun and turn it into electrical energy to power the satellite's radio. The smaller satellite is a Cosmos, many of which have been launched.

How did they get there? What are they doing? How long will they stay?

Since 1957, when Russia sent up the first man-made satellite, Sputnik 1, several hundreds of satellites have gone into orbit, fired from Earth by rockets. Some have stayed in orbit ever since. Others have returned to Earth.

Communications satellites stay in orbit to bounce radio and television signals and telephone conversations from one side of the world to the other. In this way a viewer in Australia can see an event taking place in New York while it is happening.

Weather satellites take pictures of cloud patterns above the Earth and send the information back by radio. These pictures help weather forecasters to warn people in advance of approaching bad weather.

'Spy' satellites keep a watch on the world's armies and navies. Any sudden movement of troops or ships is reported to governments.

Satellites are launched into space by rockets. But once they are in orbit, they need no engines to keep them going round. The pull of the Earth takes them round with it. In space there is no friction or other force to slow them down. They can stay in orbit for years.

Sometimes, however, scientists put instruments or cameras into satellites and want them back. These satellites are fitted with small rockets which can fire them out of orbit and back towards Earth. As a returning satellite approaches the ground, a parachute opens to let it down gently.

When a satellite launch is planned, experts know exactly where they want it

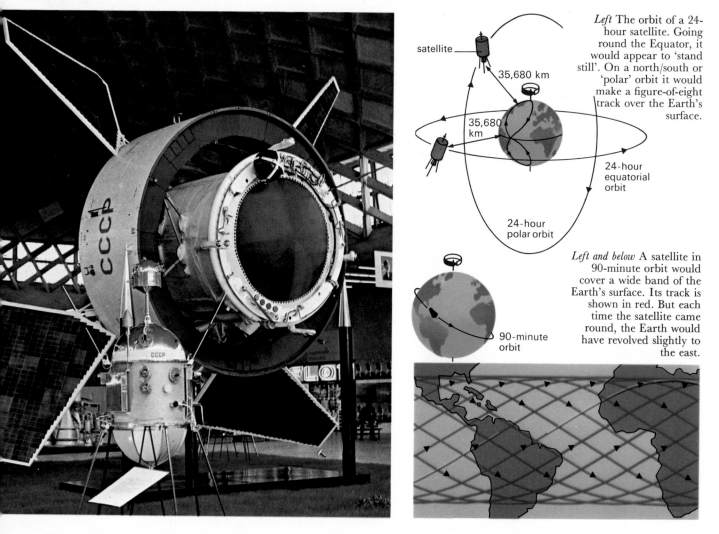

satellite

35,680 km

35,680 km

Left The orbit of a 24-hour satellite. Going round the Equator, it would appear to 'stand still'. On a north/south or 'polar' orbit it would make a figure-of-eight track over the Earth's surface.

24-hour equatorial orbit

24-hour polar orbit

90-minute orbit

Left and below A satellite in 90-minute orbit would cover a wide band of the Earth's surface. Its track is shown in red. But each time the satellite came round, the Earth would have revolved slightly to the east.

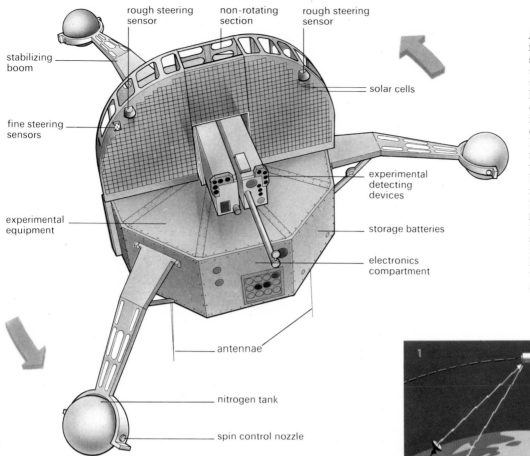

rough steering sensor

non-rotating section

rough steering sensor

stabilizing boom

fine steering sensors

solar cells

experimental detecting devices

experimental equipment

storage batteries

electronics compartment

antennae

nitrogen tank

spin control nozzle

Left A satellite launched from the United States to study the sun's rays. Like the Russian satellite on the opposite page this one has solar cells to provide electricity for the instruments. The satellite can be controlled from Earth so that its solar cells remain facing the sun, while the lower part can be made to revolve. Tape-recorders are also fitted so that the information gathered can be stored until the space centre sends a signal to 'ask' for it. The three 'legs' help to keep the satellite steady while the instruments are at work.

to go. If they want it to go round the Earth quickly–perhaps once every ninety minutes–they put it into orbit a few hundred kilometres up. If they want it to go round once a day, its orbit must be higher.

Imagine that you are in the garden with a dog on a lead. The dog is running round you. If he's on a short lead, he will get round faster. On a longer lead he will have further to run.

If you are to avoid getting tangled up with the lead, you will have to turn at the same speed as the dog. With a short lead you'll have to turn very fast indeed. By lengthening the lead you can go more slowly.

A satellite moving at the same speed as the Earth will always stay above the same point on the Earth's surface. It will appear to be 'standing still' in space. Communications satellites are of this type.

Such satellites take twenty-four hours to make a complete orbit. During the same time the Earth has turned round exactly once. But the Earth is also swinging from side to side as it goes round, and the track of the satellite in space has to be planned to allow for this. No wonder satellite launches have to be planned so carefully!

Right Three ways in which satellites are used. In 1 *(top)* a communications satellite is relaying telephone conversations between Britain and America. Such satellites can deal with hundreds of calls at the same time.

In 2 *(middle)* another kind of communications satellite sends out position signals to ships and aircraft.

In 3 *(bottom)* a weather satellite takes pictures of cloud formations in slightly overlapping areas. When these pictures are relayed back to Earth, weathermen can build up a total picture of world weather.

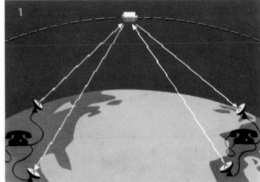

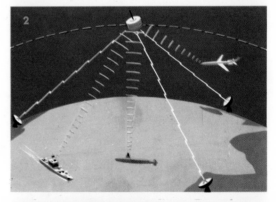

31

The radiotelescope

On a clear night you can see hundreds of stars without using a telescope. With even an ordinary, cheap telescope you can see many more. But if you used the best telescope in the world, you couldn't see everything that there is in space.

The stars that you can see send out light-waves. But not all the waves travelling through space are light-waves. Many are radio-waves. Some of these are sent out by stars, and some by objects that no one can see. The radio-waves are too weak to be picked up by an ordinary radio set. They can be received only by a radiotelescope.

An ordinary radio receives signals from a powerful transmitter and turns the signals into sounds. A radiotelescope works in a similar way. But because the signals it picks up are so weak, it has a huge aerial to make the signals stronger and clearer. The aerial is the thing you notice first about a radiotelescope. Some aerials are dish-shaped. They make the signals easier to pick up, just as if you cup your hand round your ear you can hear more clearly what someone is saying a long way off. Other radio-telescopes have arrangements of wires stretched out across the ground.

With the help of a radiotelescope a radio-astronomer can make a 'radio map' of the universe. The aerial can be tilted in any direction so that he can concentrate on any particular part of the sky. When the signals come in from space, they can be turned into sounds or into pictures like those on a radar screen. They can be recorded and played back later for closer study.

Some of the signals have been travelling through space for millions of years. They are so weak that one radiotelescope on its own may not be able to pin-point them accurately. So two or more radiotelescopes are sometimes used together. In this way a more accurate 'fix' of a signal's position can be made.

What sort of signals does a radiotelescope pick up? First, there are signals that come from familiar objects in the universe like the sun and the planet Jupiter. Then there are signals from

Below One of the world's largest radiotelescopes is at Jodrell Bank, near Manchester in England. Its dish-shaped aerial is 76 metres across. It can be tilted up and down and from left to right to point in any direction that scientists want to study.

light is a strange colour, quite unlike the light from anything else in the universe. Scientists are still arguing about what quasars are. Some think that they are bits of stars from our own galaxy which have broken off and are hurtling away from us at high speed. Others believe that quasars are not solid objects at all but simply masses of energy.

One exciting possibility is that radio-telescopes may one day pick up signals sent out not by stars or pulsars but by intelligent beings somewhere in space. If this happened, it would change man's whole view of life, just as the radiotelescope has already changed his ideas on the universe.

Left A cross-shaped radiotelescope aerial at Medicina, near Bologna in Italy.

objects that send out no light-waves and which we cannot see. There are whole galaxies–'radio galaxies'–that no one knew about before the radiotelescope was invented.

Radio-astronomy is a very new science. It was started in 1931. But already scientists have discovered many new objects in the sky. As more powerful radiotelescopes are built, they pick up more and more objects far out in space. Some of their discoveries are mysteries.

Among these are 'pulsars'. In 1968 radio-astronomers working with a new radiotelescope at Cambridge, in England, heard what sounded like a regular ticking sound. It came over the loudspeakers every one and one-third second like the ticking of a clock. Did this mean, the scientists wondered, that someone out in space was trying to get in touch with Earth?

After other radiotelescopes had picked up similar signals, it was decided that, although they sounded man-made because they were so regular, the signals were natural. It was also noticed that some pulsars gave out flashes, or 'pulses' of light, at the same time as the radio signals.

No one has yet decided exactly what pulsars are. But one idea is that they are tiny stars which are dying and cooling down. As they spin very fast in space, they send out radio and sometimes light signals from spots of energy still left alive on the surface.

Even more mysterious are 'quasars', also discovered by the radiotelescope. These give out radio- and light-waves, and sometimes X-rays as well. But the

Left The quasar 3C-273, which was discovered in 1963 by the Dutch astronomer Maarten Schmidt, working at the Mount Palomar Observatory in California, USA. This is an ordinary photograph taken through the Mount Palomar telescope, but as well as light rays quasar 3C-273 also sends out radio signals and X-rays.

Below The first pulsar to be discovered. It was found in a big cloud of gas called the Crab nebula. Numbered NP0532, it ticks out a radio signal and flashes light about thirty times a second.

Left It was at this giant radiotelescope just outside Cambridge, England, that pulsars were first discovered. The radiotelescope has two aerials. This is the smaller one, about sixty metres in length, which is mounted on rails so that it can be moved into the best position for work. The second aerial is approximately five hundred metres long.

Below Another radiotelescope dish, this time at Effelburg in Germany. The cars on the road below show how huge it is. The dish can turn up and down on the crane-like structure which supports it, and the whole radiotelescope can be revolved on a circular trackway at the base. In this way the dish can be made to point to any part of the sky.

The telescope

It was about 700 years ago that the discovery was made that rays of light could be bent by letting them pass through different shapes of glass. All optical instruments—telescopes, microscopes, magnifying glasses, cameras, film and slide projectors, spectacles and many more—make use of this discovery.

Telescopes are arrangements of lenses and sometimes mirrors which make objects look closer than they really are.

To understand how telescopes work it's easiest to start with the most simple type, which uses only lenses. In the top diagram on the opposite page you can see a convex lens drawn from the side. As the light rays from an object pass through it, they are bent towards one another. They cross over and make an image—a copy of the object. If, instead of a convex lens, a piece of plain glass were used, the light rays would pass straight through. The action of the lens pulling the rays together is called focusing.

A lens makes objects look bigger because the light rays meeting it are spread out over a wide area. Because of the curve of the lens, it is further from the light rays from the top to those from the bottom of the object than it would be if the glass were plain.

The 'objective' lens—the one nearest the object—is at one end of the telescope.

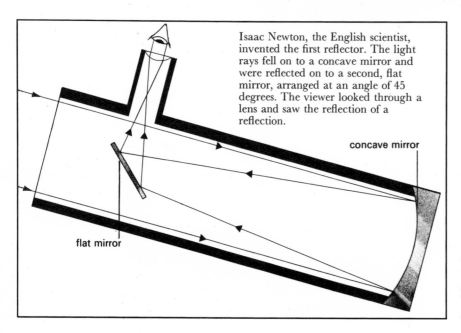

Isaac Newton, the English scientist, invented the first reflector. The light rays fell on to a concave mirror and were reflected on to a second, flat mirror, arranged at an angle of 45 degrees. The viewer looked through a lens and saw the reflection of a reflection.

concave mirror

flat mirror

At the other end is the eyepiece, which enables the viewer to see the image. After the light rays have passed through the objective lens, the image is upside down. In a telescope made for looking at the stars and planets this doesn't matter, because there is no 'right way up' in the sky. But most telescopes of this kind might also be used to look at distant objects across country or at sea, so an extra lens is used to turn the image round once more and present it to the viewer 'right way up'.

This kind of telescope is called a 'refractor', and if you have a pocket telescope it will work like this. But in order to get really close-up views through a refractor you need a very long and clumsy tube between the lenses. Telescopes in observatories are of a different type, called 'reflectors'.

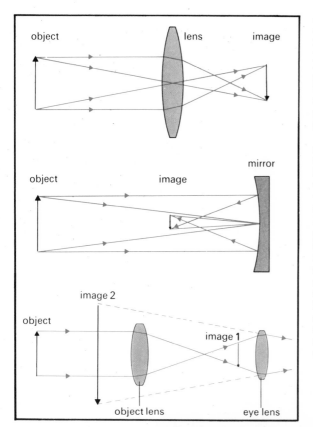

object	lens	image

| object | image | mirror |

image 2

object

image 1

object lens

eye lens

Left The job of any kind of telescope is to present a nearer, clearer image of the object to the observer. In the refractor in the top diagram the light rays are bent by a convex lens and turned upside down, making an upside-down image. In the refractor *(middle)* the rays are reflected by the mirror twice, making the object look even closer. Either way an image is formed which the observer sees through his eyepiece *(bottom diagram)*. The problem faced by early inventors of telescopes was that glass in those days could not be made well enough to cut out possible distortions of the image. Nowadays it is possible to make glass that bends or reflects rays of light exactly, with no distortions.

A reflector uses a mirror as well as a lens to collect and present the image. An ordinary mirror makes an object seem twice as far away as it really is. A concave mirror makes it seem even further away, because the light rays can bounce on to it, away again, back again and away before they make an image. You can see how this happens in the middle diagram on this page. The image is seen through an eyepiece, as in a refractor, and as reflectors are usually used for studying the night sky, there is no need to worry about whether the viewer sees the object upside down or not.

In large modern telescopes it is not necessary to peer through an eyepiece. The image can be projected on to a screen, so that the viewer can sit comfortably and watch it, or on to a film, so that a photograph can be taken. The pictures of the night sky on the next two pages were taken in this way.

Left The dome of the Hale reflector telescope at Mount Palomar observatory in California. The dome and the telescope itself can be turned to point to any part of the night sky that astronomers wish to study.

Right Inside the dome of the Hale reflector at Mount Palomar. The telescope's size can be estimated from the size of the people on the floor below. This is one of the largest telescopes in the world, and it is designed so that the images it produces can be either observed at the time or recorded on film. The 'objective' end is at the top right of the picture. Observers can work in the cage at the top left. The whole telescope can move in two planes–vertically, by means of the horseshoe-shaped mounting on the right, and horizontally, by means of a pivot at the base.

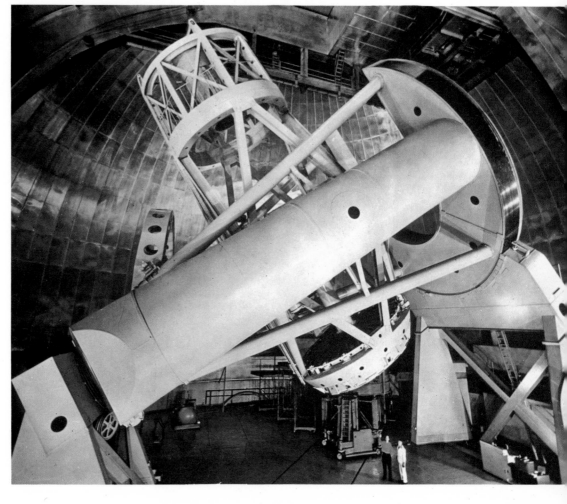

Right The Mount Palomar observatory in California contains a number of different telescopes. One of them, the 120 cm Schmidt reflector, took this picture of the star cluster Pleiades, which from Earth, to the naked eye, looks like a group of six very faint stars. The photograph shows that in addition to the six stars that we can see there are many more that, even through a powerful telescope, look like mere pin-points of light. The light rays captured from the six main stars of Pleiades started their journey about 400 years ago. The light from the others comes from even longer ago.

Below left The galaxy of Andromeda Spiral, showing how the state of heavenly bodies is always in the process of change. The centre of the galaxy is the large object to the centre right of the picture. The second object *(top left)* is a mixture of gas and dust.

In time the gas and dust will form a new galaxy. But it takes millions of years for this to happen. The night sky still looks very much the same to us as it looked to the first human beings on Earth about half a million years ago.

Below right Although man has been studying the stars for hundreds of years, they are still a mystery. These are quasars–stars which give out pulses of radio-waves. How can a quite small object give out enough energy to be seen from Earth millions of miles away? This is a question astronomers are trying to answer.

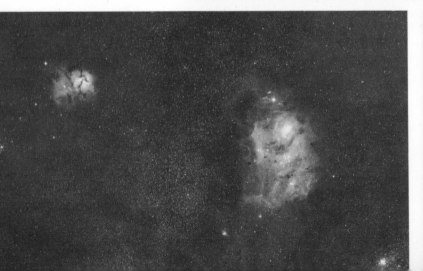

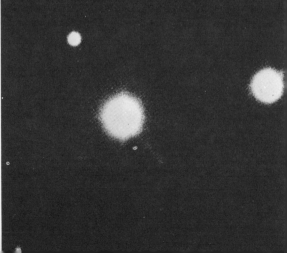

Below left Part of the constellation Hercules, millions of light-years across.
Below right A cloud of hydrogen gas and dust 6,000 light-years away from Earth, photographed by the Mount Palomar observatory. The gas—a dull red—glows because it takes in light from the nearby stars. From the swirling mass of gas, astronomers think, will come the stars of the future. But they will not be seen in the lifetime of anyone now on Earth. The making of new stars takes millions of years.

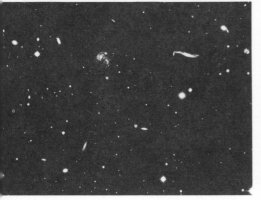

A planetarium

A planetarium is a moving map of the universe shown on a screen inside the dome of a building. It is arranged so that a true picture of the sky, for any part of the world and at any point in time, can be shown.

Although a visit to a planetarium makes a good outing, what you will see there is scientifically correct as well as being a good show. Because it is all done by mirrors, lenses and very accurate machinery, the movement of the stars and planets can be speeded up so that you can watch the whole year's star movements in a few minutes. Even if

Below At the London Planetarium the projector picks out the shape of the constellation Cygnus, the Swan, that star-watchers used to imagine they could see in the sky. At the bottom left of the picture the image of the Sun can be seen 'setting' behind the London skyline.

you visited the most powerful laboratory in the world, you couldn't learn so much about the sky in such a short time.

The demonstrations in a planetarium are arranged in programmes. One day you might be able, for example, to see a total eclipse of the Sun, when the Moon blots out the Sun's light. Another day you might see a whole year or more's star movements speeded up. While the programme is going on, a demonstrator explains what is happening.

A planetarium is really a model of the universe made out of points of light. No model made out of fixed objects would be as good. The secret is in the projector—the instrument that stands in the centre of a planetarium looking rather like a huge insect. The large knobs at each end of the projector are the 'star globes'—one showing the stars

of the Northern hemisphere, the other those of the Southern. Inside each star globe is a powerful electric lamp. The light from this is projected on to the ceiling through a series of lenses which form images of the forty-two brightest fixed stars, three variable stars, the Milky Way, the Sun, the Moon and each of the planets, as well as over 8,000 other stars.

Separate parts of the planetarium projector are movable, so that the Moon, the Sun and the planets, for example, can move independently across the background of the fixed stars. In addition, the projector moves in order to imitate the movements of the Earth. When the yearly motion of the Earth round the Sun is being demonstrated, the dumb-bell formed by the two globes rotates around the line joining the globes. All the stars are carried round

Right The three ways in which the planetarium projector can move. 'Precessional motion' is the slow wobbling of the Earth round its axis.
Below A modern planetarium projector, showing the globes and separate 'star projectors'.

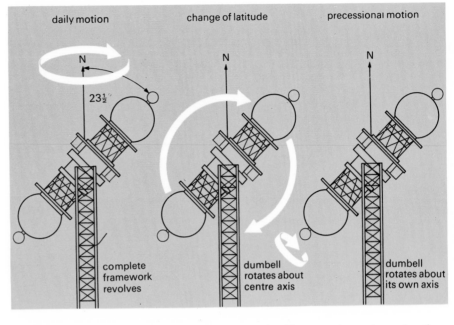

daily motion   change of latitude   precessional motion

N   N   N

$23\frac{1}{2}$

complete framework revolves

dumbell rotates about centre axis

dumbell rotates about its own axis

the planetarium's 'sky' by this motion. When the daily motion of the Earth – its spinning movement – is being demonstrated, the dumb-bell turns with the complete framework on a vertical axis. For a demonstration involving a 'pretend' journey north or south to see what the sky looks like from there, the dumbbell can be swung to point further up or down.

As well as showing the sky as it really looks – or rather, as it would really look if the lights of cities and atmospheric pollution did not spoil the view for us – the planetarium can show 'special effects'. A special small globe mounted on each of the star globes can project the names and outlines of the constellations. This is what is happening in the picture opposite. The projector is showing how the constellation Cygnus, the Swan, got its name.

Although many planetaria are fitted out like cinemas, with comfortable seats and all the feeling of going to a show, they are not toys. As well as teaching us about the movements of the stars and planets they also enable scientists to 'look back' to various times in the history of the universe to see what was happening then, or to 'look forward' to see what will happen in future. The planetarium can show us, for example, that in 12,000 years' time the Earth will have a different Pole-Star. The axis on which the Earth spins 'wobbles' so that it points to different parts of the sky at different times. At present it points to Polaris, the Pole-Star. But in 12,000 years from now it will have wobbled so that it will then point to Vega, a brilliant star in the constellation of the Lyre. Vega will then be our Pole-Star.

Thousands of accurate calculations are needed to work out the movements that a planetarium projector must make. In modern planetaria these calculations are made by computers, which also control the actual movements of the projector's various parts. In the article on computers you can read that information given to a computer may be stored on magnetic tape and replayed when it is needed. Programmes for different planetarium shows can be made up and kept in this way. They can be played back so that the computer tape 'tells' the projector what movements to make. The demonstrator's commentary on the programme can also, of course, be recorded.

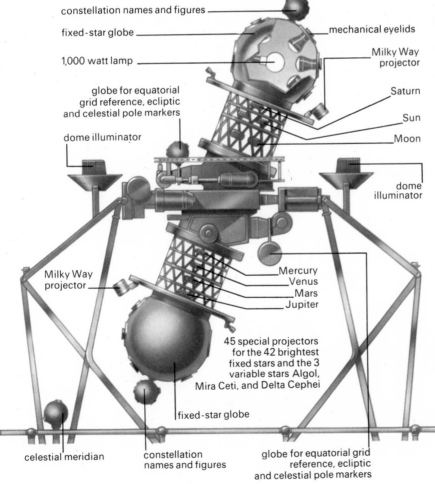

constellation names and figures

fixed-star globe

1,000 watt lamp

globe for equatorial grid reference, ecliptic and celestial pole markers

dome illuminator

mechanical eyelids

Milky Way projector

Saturn

Sun

Moon

dome illuminator

Milky Way projector

Mercury
Venus
Mars
Jupiter

45 special projectors for the 42 brightest fixed stars and the 3 variable stars Algol, Mira Ceti, and Delta Cephei

fixed-star globe

celestial meridian

constellation names and figures

globe for equatorial grid reference, ecliptic and celestial pole markers

Hovercraft and hydrofoils

Ships are among the oldest forms of transport used by man, but no one has ever succeeded in making them go really fast. Even with the most modern types of engines few ships can travel at more than about 50 kph, and most are much slower than that.

The reason is that water resists anything passing through it. If you are a swimmer, you will know that it takes an enormous amount of energy to swim really fast. The resistance of the water is dragging you back all the time. Ships have the same trouble, and the bigger the ship, the greater the resistance of the water to it. There is little chance that ordinary ships will ever be able to travel much faster than they do now. And even in the most powerful ships most of the energy from the engines is wasted in fighting the drag of the water.

If a boat can be lifted just above the water and made to skim the waves instead of ploughing through them, the problem of the drag of the water disappears. Speedboats are able to reach high speeds (although only for short distances) because when they are travelling fast only a small part of their hulls is actually touching the water. Hovercraft and hydrofoils both use the idea of lifting the hull out of the water to beat the water's drag.

The hovercraft was invented by a British engineer, Sir Christopher Cockerell. His idea was to mount a fan on top of a specially shaped hull and so pump a jet of air downwards to lift the hovercraft off the surface. This makes a cushion of air underneath the hull. The air leaks out a little at a time, and more is pumped in from above. The sides of the 'cushion'–the 'skirt'–may be made of stiff rubber or formed by a 'curtain' of air-jets.

Hovercraft can travel just as easily over land as on water, and seagoing hovercraft dock simply by drawing up on to the beach. This means that they can be very quickly loaded and un-

Right Air is drawn in at the top of a hovercraft by a fan and pumped down to form a cushion underneath. It escapes between the bottom of the skirt and the surface of the sea.
Below One of the Seaspeed hovercraft with which British Rail operates services across the English Channel. This craft carries cars as well as passengers.

loaded without all the trouble of docking in a harbour. Hovercraft are useful for quick journeys across short stretches of water like the English Channel, which thousands of tourists cross during the summer. Because they do the trip more quickly than an ordinary cross-Channel ferry, they carry more passengers and cars each day than a shipping service could manage.

At sea hovercraft can travel at up to 160 kph. Special hovercraft have also been built for use by troops. With their help an army need no longer hold up its advance or retreat while a river bridge is built or repaired.

The forward movement in a hovercraft is provided by propeller engines which work in the air, not under water

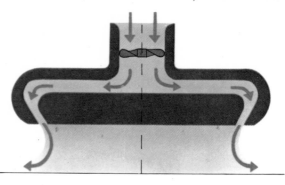

as in an ordinary ship. Because there is little resistance from the water, these engines need not be as powerful as ships' engines and do not use as much fuel either.

Unlike the hovercraft, a hydrofoil at rest in the water looks just like an ordinary ship. Its decks and hull are boat-shaped. But underneath the water it has sets of foils—shaped pieces of metal rather like aircraft wings.

When the hydrofoil sets off, it quickly builds up speed and the hull rises up out of the water, carried along by the foils which skim across the surface rather like surf-boards. Because there is so little contact between the foils and the water, there is very little drag, and high speeds

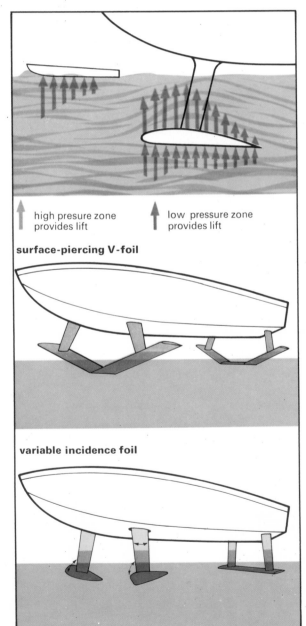

Left On the left of the diagram the hull of an ordinary boat is kept up by the pressure of water from below. On the right a hydrofoil and its foil. Water passes more quickly over the foil than underneath, creating low pressure on top. Pressure from below pushes the foil up, and the hull to which it is attached rises.

Left The large V-shaped foils of this hydrofoil help to steady it.

Left In this type of hydrofoil the angle of the foils can be altered to suit different conditions at sea. This can make the journey smoother in rough weather.

Above The front foil of a hydrofoil emerges from the water as the vessel speeds up. Like an ordinary ship it is propeller-driven, but the propeller shaft is arranged vertically so that it remains submerged even when the hull is lifted out of the water.

can be reached. Unlike an ordinary ship, a hydrofoil leaves no wake or 'wash' behind it, and so it is particularly useful for providing transport along rivers and canals where the wake of ordinary ships could damage the banks.

The foils work exactly like aircraft wings. They are curved so that water takes longer to pass over them than underneath. The water underneath is at greater pressure and so pushes the foil up towards the surface.

Hydrofoils are used mainly for passenger services in fairly calm stretches of water. There is just one problem. They can travel faster than any ordinary ship but they are in danger of breaking up if they go at more than about 100 kph. This is because the drag of the water becomes too great for the foils to stand.

For the same reason it is not easy to design hydrofoils able to stand up to the battering of waves in the open ocean. Naval designers are at work on the problem, however, because hydrofoils, with their extra speed, would make useful submarine hunter-killers. One hydrofoil built for this purpose is already in use by the Royal Canadian Navy. When it is searching for submarines, it cruises along in the usual way, as an ordinary ship. But if an enemy sub is sighted, the hydrofoil speeds up and closes in on its victim faster than any submarine can escape.

The submarine

Submarines are built for only one reason: for war. Lurking under the surface of the sea, they can carry out with complete surprise an attack on an enemy's navy or merchant ships. Modern submarines with nuclear-powered engines can stay submerged for long periods. One US Navy nuclear-powered submarine, the *Triton,* stayed down long enough to sail right round the world without coming to the surface once.

Submarines have propellers to drive them and rudders to steer them, just like other ships. But they also need to sink and rise, dive and climb in the water. To achieve this their designers use the principle of buoyancy.

Air is lighter than water, and a quantity of air inside a sealed vessel will keep it afloat. But if the air is taken out and replaced with water, the vessel will sink. This is how a submarine works. Inside its hull it has buoyancy tanks –large steel-lined tanks which run most of the way from bow to stern. When the submarine is on the surface of the sea, the tanks contain air which helps it to float. To make the vessel sink the tanks are filled with sea water. When the submarine is at the level the captain has chosen, some of the water is blown out of the tanks by compressed air. Then the submarine has 'neutral buoyancy'–just enough water in the tanks to keep it submerged and just

enough air to stop it sinking any deeper. The flow of water is controlled by valves and this can be measured very accurately.

As well as the main buoyancy tanks there are smaller 'trim tanks' with which fine adjustments to the buoyancy can be made. As fuel is used up on the voyage, for example, water is pumped into the trim tanks to give weight in place of the fuel.

Used on their own the buoyancy tanks would submerge or surface the submarine fairly slowly. Often a submarine has to move fast. To help them do this they are fitted with hydroplanes–pairs of wings like short aircraft wings which stick out sideways

Left A submarine cruising on the surface.
Below How the space is used in a typical submarine. The spaces in the bottom of the hull are the buoyancy tanks, which also surround the living quarters and engine compartments on the sides and on top. Submarine crews are trained to live in cramped quarters and to move about with the least disturbance to things around them.

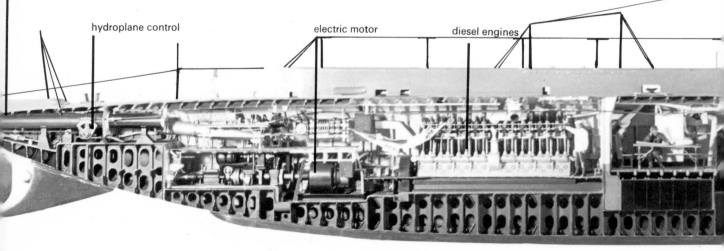

rear torpedo tube

hydroplane control

electric motor

diesel engines

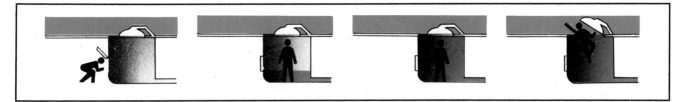

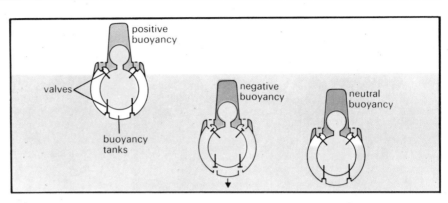

Above How the escape-hatch works. As the air is pumped out, water is pumped in until the pressure inside the chamber equals that of the sea outside. Then the escaper opens the top hatch and is free.

Right 'Positive buoyancy' keeps the submarine on the surface when the buoyancy tanks are full of air. As water is pumped in, the submarine sinks. This is 'negative buoyancy'. By mixing the proportions of air and water in the buoyancy tanks the submarine can be kept in 'neutral buoyancy'. Then it will stay at the chosen level.

from the hull. The hydroplanes can be tilted forwards or backwards, and the water pressure acting on their surfaces gives the submarine extra 'lift' or 'fall' in just the same way as the wings of an aircraft. When the submarine is moving on a level track at speed, the hydroplanes can be drawn into the hull so that they do not 'drag' in the water.

Submarines are fitted with radar and other devices so that their crews know what is going on above them on the surface of the sea. But they can also 'see out' by means of the periscope. This is an arrangement of mirrors and lenses which can be raised so that it sticks up above the water. The top lens and mirror catch the view from above and send it down the periscope tube where it is picked up by the bottom mirror and

presented through the eyepiece to the viewer. The periscope tube can be turned through 360 degrees so that the viewer can obtain an all-round view while the hull of the submarine is still safely hidden beneath the waves.

If a submarine is damaged under water, it may be unable to surface. The crew must then escape through the escape-hatch.

It would be no good having a simple hatch which opened to let the crew out. Water would flood in and drown anyone left inside the submarine. So submarine escape-hatches are 'airlocks', with two airtight and watertight doors. The escaping crew member climbs from the submarine into the airlock and shuts the door behind him. The air in the chamber is sucked out and sea water

pumped in. When the chamber is full of water, the escaper opens the top hatch and swims out, striking out hard for the surface. The top hatch is closed again, and the water is pumped out of the chamber. Then it is ready for the next escaper. In modern submarines the airlock can accommodate several sailors at a time.

The submarine's main weapons are torpedoes, which are fired from torpedo tubes set into the hull at the bows and stern. Torpedo tubes, too, work on the airlock principle. They are loaded from inside with hatches across the front end to keep the sea out. Then hatches at the back are closed, and the tubes, with the torpedoes inside them, flooded with sea water. The torpedoes are then ready to be fired.

Underwater exploration

Deep down in the ocean the pressure of the water is so enormous that no diver in a diving-suit could stand it. Even a submarine would be crushed as if it were made of tin foil. The limit for submarines is a depth of about 450 metres.

Anyone who wants to explore the ocean underwater at any greater depth has to use a special vessel. Many different types have been tried, but two of the best-known and most successful are the bathyscaphe and the bathysphere. The 'bathy' part of their names comes from the ancient Greek word for 'deep'.

The bathyscaphe has dived deeper into the ocean than any other vessel. In 1960 two men—the inventor Jacques Piccard, and a US Navy officer—made a record dive of over 10,000 metres.

The bathyscaphe is built of immensely thick steel plates to withstand the underwater pressure. At the bottom is a metal globe with a porthole in which the

crew travels. Above this is a large float which is filled with petrol. There are also tanks into which iron balls are loaded.

The weight of the iron balls carries the bathyscaphe down. In Jacques Piccard's record-breaking bathyscaphe *Trieste* there was a small motor-driven propeller which enabled the vessel to move about under the ocean. When the crew have carried out their research, they unload the iron balls into the sea. With the weight lightened the petrol, which is lighter than water, pulls the bathyscaphe back to the surface. All the bathyscaphe's movements have to be made slowly and carefully. When Piccard made his 10,000-metre dive, it took him five hours to go down and over three hours to return. That's about half a metre every second going down, and one metre every second coming up.

The bathysphere cannot go as deep,

because it must always stay connected with a ship on the surface which lowers and raises it on a cable. There is also a telephone line to the surface so that the bathysphere's crew can record their notes. Like the bathyscaphe, the bathysphere is immensely strong, with thick portholes through which the crew can observe their underwater surroundings. It carries its own oxygen supply and chemicals to absorb the poisonous carbon dioxide that the crew breathes out.

The record descent for a bathysphere was 1,370 metres, which was achieved by Dr Otis Barton off Santa Cruz, California, in 1949.

Opposite The bathysphere *Purisima*, built for underwater exploration in the United States. Unlike the bathyscaphe the bathysphere must remain tethered to its 'mother ship' while it is under water. It has no means of raising itself under its own power. Note the cable at the top which provides lift and a phone link.

Below The bathyscaphe *Trieste* in which Jacques Piccard and Lt Walsh of the US Navy made their record underwater descent of over 10,000 metres in 1960. The crew's quarters are in the globe at the bottom of the vessel. The tanks above are for the petrol supply which brings the bathyscaphe back to the surface, and for the iron balls which are loaded on board to make it descend and unloaded into the sea for the upward journey.

sea level
frogman
diving suit
submarine
bathysphere

bathyscaphe
35,800 ft

deepest known
ocean floor

PURISIMA

OFFSHORE DIVERS · UNION CARBIDE
OCEAN SYSTEMS · GENERAL
INC. · PRECISION

Scuba-diving

Without some kind of special diving gear even the best divers can stay under the water for only two or three minutes. After that, they have to come back to the surface to breathe.

But there are all sorts of reasons why someone may want to stay under water for longer than a few minutes. He may want to explore a wreck at the bottom of the sea or to observe deep-sea marine life. He may have to carry out repairs to a ship's hull or to an oil-rig. Or he may just want to explore underwater for fun.

With a deep-sea diving-suit a man can reach depths of about 180 metres. A diving-suit has its own pressure so that the diver can withstand the huge pressure on him from the water. There are strong glass windows in the helmet, and the diver is supplied with air from a line to a ship on the surface. The line also carries a telephone link.

Diving-suits like this are clumsy and expensive. The diver must always remain connected with the surface. He must wear heavy boots to keep him upright, and these make him move slowly and awkwardly.

Left This scuba-diver is using a small underwater craft with a propeller. It enables him to cover a very much wider area than would otherwise be possible in the two hours or so that he can stay below before his air supply runs out. There is also room for him to store specimens that he picks up on his way.

Above A wet-suited scuba-diver ready to explore deep under the surface. His gear includes a radio with which he can communicate with the surface, using the microphone strapped to his right leg. Clipped to his belt is a powerful torch, because some parts of the sea are so full of tiny creatures that they are almost pitch dark.

Above A scuba-diver explores the wreck of a ship that sank hundreds of years ago. Underwater archaeologists have discovered many of the secrets of the sailors of long ago.

When his work is over, he must return to the surface slowly, if he surfaces too quickly, he may suffer from a painful and dangerous illness called the 'bends'. The nitrogen in the air he breathes is taken into his blood instead of being breathed out. If he comes back too soon, the nitrogen bubbles stay in his veins and may even kill him.

All these problems are overcome in scuba-diving. 'Scuba' stands for Self-Contained Underwater Breathing Apparatus. The scuba-diver takes his own air with him in metal bottles strapped to his back. He can go almost as deep as a man in a diving-suit, and he can move about much more freely because there is no line connecting him with the surface and his gear is lighter.

The air bottles are connected by tube with the diver's mouth. There is a valve in the tube so that he can control how much air he breathes. The 'air' is a mixture of oxygen and helium. It con-

tains no nitrogen, so the scuba-diver is in no danger from the 'bends' when he comes up.

As well as his air supply the scuba-diver wears flippers and a rubber face-mask with a window for his eyes. He may also wear a wet suit made of rubber. This does not fit him tightly. Between his skin and the rubber of the suit is a space which is filled with water. The diver's body warms the water and provides a layer of warmth between him and the cold water outside.

This leaves the diver's hands free to work tools or a camera or shine a torch. A scuba-diver can stay down fifty or so metres below the surface for up to two hours. Some have been as deep as 120 metres, and the record scuba-dive was 210 metres. But at these depths the water pressure is too great for safety.

The breathing apparatus used by the scuba-diver is called an 'aqualung'. It was invented during World War II by the French underwater scientist Jacques Cousteau, who has made many films about life under the sea. Because they can move silently and get about more easily than ordinary divers, scuba-

divers found plenty of work in wartime, fixing mines to sabotage enemy ships and even enemy harbours. They were also used to make quick underwater surveys of damaged ships.

Many people go scuba-diving just for fun. They like to explore the depths and observe or photograph the wildlife that they see down there. Others are interested in finding old wrecks and recovering parts of their cargo. Thanks to scuba-diving we now know a great deal about the ships of the ancient empires of Greece and Rome and the sort of goods they carried.

But for some other people scuba-diving is a way of earning a living. The captain of a ship may want a diver to inspect the hull beneath the water-line. There may be work to be done on the piles that hold up a pier. Police forces train 'frogmen' to search lakes and rivers for stolen property that has been dumped, or for the bodies of murder victims. In his scuba gear a man can move under water almost as easily as if he had been born with fins and a tail.

The steam locomotive

There are many people who believe that the only *real* railways are those where the trains are hauled by steam locomotives. There is certainly something very exciting about a steam train going at full speed, leaving a cloud of steam and smoke and the smell of burning coal behind it.

There are still a few countries, such as India, where railways are run by steam, but in most places your only chance of a ride on a steam-hauled train is to visit one of the lines that have been kept open as museums. The railways were built for steam, however, and were run mainly by steam for a hundred years. During that time steam-engines also provided the power for factories, waterworks, ships and even, in traction-engines, for road vehicles.

Like petrol and diesel engines steam-engines have pistons which move up and down inside closely fitting cylinders. The piston is connected at one end to a piston-rod which moves to and fro through a hole in the end of the cylinder.

The piston-rod is connected to the locomotive's driving-wheels in an arrangement similar to a bicycle's pedal-wheel. If a bicycle's pedals stuck out of

Left This was one of the last British steam locomotives to be built. The very last was No. 92220 *Evening Star*, which was completed at Swindon Works on 18 March 1960. Eight years later saw the last main-line steam journey on Britain's railway system, from Liverpool to Carlisle. In Britain and many other countries steam locomotives can be seen only on short lengths of track run by railway preservation societies.

the centre of the pedal-wheel, you wouldn't be able to turn them round, but because the power of your leg muscles pushes against pedals mounted on extra 'spokes' the wheel is forced round. In the same way the piston-rod of a steam locomotive is connected to the driving-wheels so that its to-and-fro movement is changed into a circular one.

The energy that makes the piston move in its cylinder is provided by steam. You will have seen how when a kettle is boiling the steam makes the lid

move up and down. This is because water expands about 1,700 times when it becomes steam. Most of a steam locomotive consists of a huge boiler in which steam is made by means of a fire, usually burning coal. The fire heats the water to make steam, and the steam is used to push the piston to and fro in the cylinder.

A great amount of steam must be produced to get a locomotive on the move and keep it going. It must all be stored and controlled. As it is made, it is channelled to the 'steamhead' at the top

Below A cutaway view of a locomotive designed for transcontinental work. The large tender, containing the water tank and coal-bunker, makes it possible for the locomotive to cover long distances before stopping to take on fresh supplies.

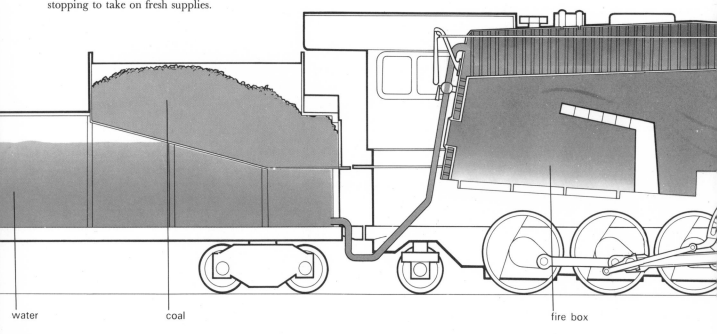

water   coal   fire box

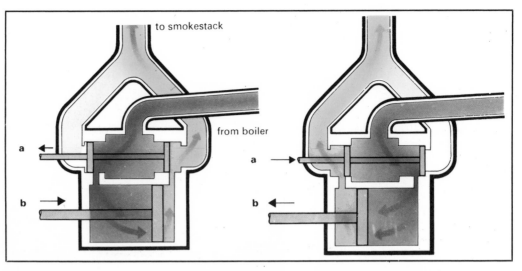

Right The sliding valve enables steam to be delivered to the cylinder on both strokes of the piston. The valve is arranged so that when one of the holes through which steam can reach the cylinder is open the other is closed. Without the valve the piston could be powered on only one of its movements. It is the escape of steam at the end of the stroke that makes the steam locomotive's distinctive 'puff-puff' sound.

of the locomotive behind the smokestack or funnel. The steamhead contains a safety-valve which 'blows' if the pressure of steam becomes too strong, and this lets some of the steam out. Inside the locomotive the steam passes into hot tubes where it is stored. It reaches the cylinder through a 'slide valve' which can move. In one position the slide valve lets steam into the bottom of the cylinder and under the piston. As it enters, the steam pushes the piston upwards. At the same time another hole in the slide valve lets steam escape from the space above the piston, in much the same way as an exhaust valve in a petrol engine. As the piston moves upwards, the slide

valve moves to a new position where it lets steam into the top of the cylinder. The hole for the steam shuts, and pressure builds up in the top part of the cylinder, pushing the piston down again.

The 'used' steam goes out of the locomotive through the funnel, which is the exhaust system.

In the hundred years when the steam locomotive was 'king of the railways' many improvements were made to it. These included a system by which the steam, instead of being pushed out of the funnel after its work was done, was sent back into the steam tubes and used again. But the sad truth is that the steam

locomotive, despite these improvements, was never very efficient. Too much of the energy it produced was wasted. It used huge amounts of coal, and keeping its boilers stoked was hard, heavy work. The noise and the soot polluted the countryside through which it passed.

As other kinds of engines were invented, especially diesels and electrics, steam became less popular. Diesels and electrics are easier to drive, cheaper to run and cheaper to maintain. So for the steam locomotive it was the end of the line.

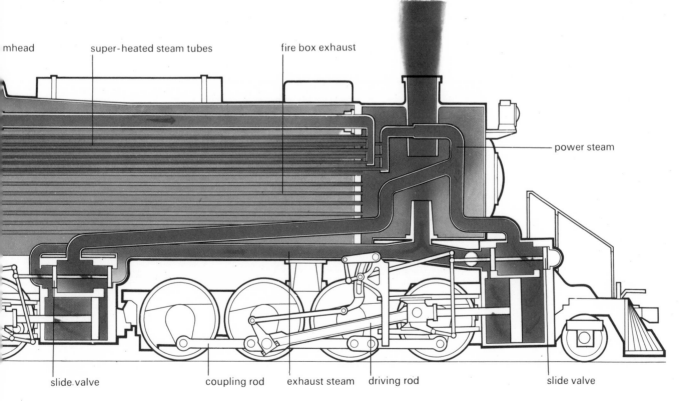

The diesel locomotive

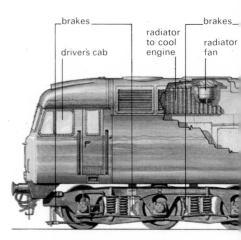

Above A diesel-electric locomotive heading the Washington to Chicago express on America's Baltimore and Ohio railroad.

The diesel engine is named after the man who invented it, a German engineer called Rudolf Diesel. Like the petrol engine of a car it is an internal combustion engine, but it works in an entirely different way.

If you have read the article about the automobile on pages 54–5, you will remember that in a petrol engine the pistons compress a mixture of petrol and air, which is then exploded by a spark from a sparking-plug. This pushes the piston along the cylinder and drives round the crankshaft to which the piston is attached.

Rudolf Diesel's first working engine went on sale in 1898, but he had been working on the idea for several years before that. The idea began when he was studying compressors–machines that press air or gas into a smaller space. He had noticed that when they were working compressors became very hot. As a gas is forced into a tight space, heat is produced. If the heat is not carried away, the temperature of the gas rises.

Diesel's idea was that if the mixture of fuel and air in an engine could be compressed really tightly it would get hot enough to explode without the help of a spark.

His first attempt to make such an engine, using coal-dust as the fuel, blew up, but Diesel was not worried. The fact that it had blown up proved that his idea was right! He tried different kinds of fuel and found that certain oils, heavier and thicker than petrol, worked best.

At first sight the inside of a diesel engine is very similar to that of an ordinary petrol engine. Both have pistons which can move up and down their cylinders, and the pistons are linked to a crankshaft from which the power is taken. But in the diesel engine there are no sparking-plugs.

The first stage in the working of a diesel engine, with the piston at the bottom of its stroke, is the blowing of air into the top part of the cylinder. A fan is used to increase the amount of air blown in. Then the exhaust valve at the top of the cylinder closes, and the piston moves up, compressing the air. When the air is compressed very tightly into the small space left at the top of the cylinder, oil is injected as a spray. The compressed air is so hot by this time that the spray of oil immediately lights it and there is an explosion. This pushes the piston down the cylinder, ready for the cycle to start all over again. At the same time the movement of the piston drives the crankshaft round. The burnt gas escapes through the exhaust-pipe.

Diesel engines are cheaper to run than those using petrol because they burn heavier oil which is less pure and less expensive. Diesels are also more efficient–that is, they do more work for a given amount of fuel. This is why diesels are used in vehicles such as trucks and buses which travel long distances, and in heavy-duty machinery like tractors and road-building equipment. But the pressures inside a diesel engine when it is working are enormous, and so it has to be very strongly made. This makes the diesel engine expensive to buy.

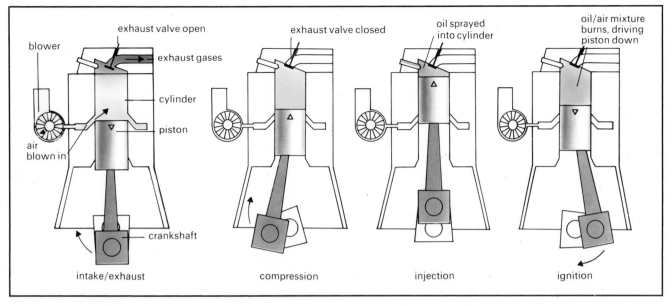

exhaust valve open
exhaust gases
blower
cylinder
piston
air blown in
crankshaft
intake/exhaust

exhaust valve closed
compression

oil sprayed into cylinder
injection

oil/air mixture burns, driving piston down
ignition

Above How a two-stroke diesel engine works. The piston comes up and squeezes the air in the cylinder, heating it to about 500°C. At the top of the piston stroke oil is injected into the cylinder. The hot mixture of oil and air burns and explodes, driving the piston down to turn the crankshaft.

Diesels also have to be maintained carefully if they are to give their best performance. If the oil is not sprayed into the cylinder at the exact second when the compression is at its greatest, there will be no explosion and the engine will fail. So regular maintenance has to be carried out to make sure that all the adjustments are correct. Thick, smoky exhaust is another sign of a badly maintained diesel engine. Not only does it annoy other road-users, but it also wastes fuel. This is why most users of diesel vehicles take them off the road frequently for checking and servicing.

The diesel engines in road vehicles transmit power direct to the driving-wheels. But when diesels are used in long-distance railway locomotives or ships, the power from the engine is used to make electricity, and it is this that drives the train or ship along. This arrangement is called the 'diesel-electric' engine.

Instead of carrying power to the driving-wheels or propellers the crank-shaft in a diesel-electric engine is connected with a dynamo. This makes electrical energy which is stored in large batteries. Power for the driving-wheels or propellers comes from electric motors, which take their current from the batteries. This may seem a round-about way of providing power but in fact it is the most efficient way when the load is a heavy one.

A long transcontinental train weighs many hundreds of tons. It takes time to reach its cruising speed and time to slow down again. If the driver were using the diesel engine directly, the huge weight of the train would be difficult to control. Electric motors, however, run more smoothly and can be controlled more carefully. In a diesel locomotive the speed of the diesel engine need not vary with the speed of the train, because the engine is providing electricity, not driving-power. This saves fuel, because diesels are most efficient when they run at a constant speed.

The advantage of diesel-electric locomotives is that as they carry their own power supply with them there is no need for an electric current to be carried along the line by a 'third rail' or overhead wire system. These systems are expensive to maintain and can easily be damaged by bad weather. Diesel-electrics are used by all the great transcontinental railways of the world such as the Canadian Pacific, the Indian Pacific line in Australia and the Trans-Siberian Railway which links eastern Europe and Asia.

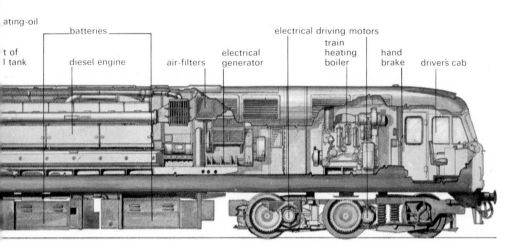

ating-oil
batteries
electrical driving motors
train heating boiler
hand brake
driver's cab
t of l tank
diesel engine
air-filters
electrical generator

Left This diesel-electric locomotive develops 2,750 horse power from its 12-cylinder diesel engine. The engine, mounted centrally, drives an electric generator which in turn feeds the storage batteries. These provide power for the electric motors fitted to the bogies.

The automobile

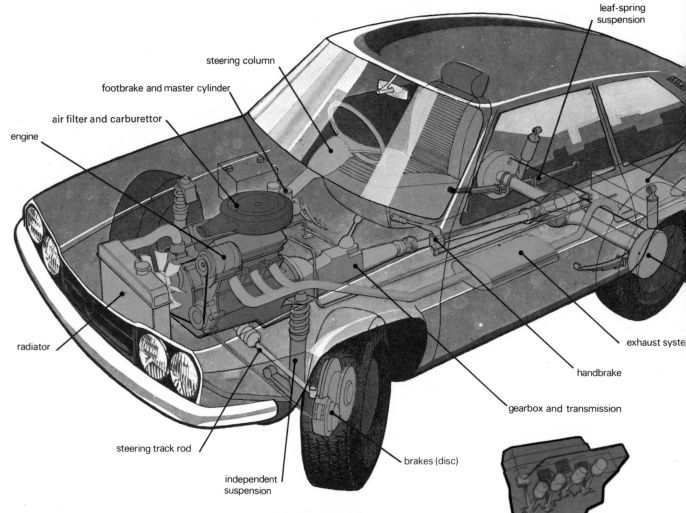

leaf-spring suspension

steering column

footbrake and master cylinder

air filter and carburettor

engine

radiator

steering track rod

independent suspension

brakes (disc)

exhaust system

handbrake

gearbox and transmission

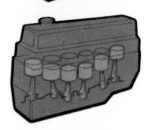

The petrol engine was invented over 100 years ago, and since then millions of automobiles powered by such engines have been built. Improvements have been made over and over again to make cars faster or safer or quieter or cheaper to run. Probably no invention has had so much attention paid to it. And you can be sure that there are more improvements to come. Despite all the changes that have been made, cars aren't as efficient as they could be.

The heart of the car is the engine, but many other parts are just as important. The steering must be safe and firm. The carburettor must feed just the right mixture of air and fuel to the engine. The gearbox and transmission carry the power of the engine to the driving-wheels. The exhaust system muffles the sound of the engine and takes the poisonous fumes under the car and out

at the back. The suspension smooths out bumps in the road and gives passengers a comfortable ride. And, of course, no car is safe without brakes!

Most internal combustion engines have pistons which move up and down inside tightly fitting cylinders. Car engines work on a four-stroke cycle. This starts with the piston at the bottom of the cylinder. The carburettor feeds a mixture of petrol and air into the top of the cylinder. The piston moves up to compress the mixture, which is exploded by a spark. The gases in the mixture expand and push the piston down again. The piston is connected to the crankshaft, which turns as the piston moves. Meanwhile, another piston in another cylinder has moved into position for the whole cycle to start all over again. The crankshaft turns part of the way round each time a cylinder is fired.

Above This car has a V-6 engine—three cylinders on each side. There are disc brakes in front and drum brakes at the rear, an arrangement which helps to avoid skidding on wet or icy roads. The radiator feeds water round the engine to cool it. The handbrake and footbrake work separately so that if one system fails the other can be used in an emergency.

The smaller diagrams show two other engine arrangements—a V-8, with two rows of four cylinders each arranged in a V-shape towards the crankshaft, and a 'straight six'—six cylinders in a line.

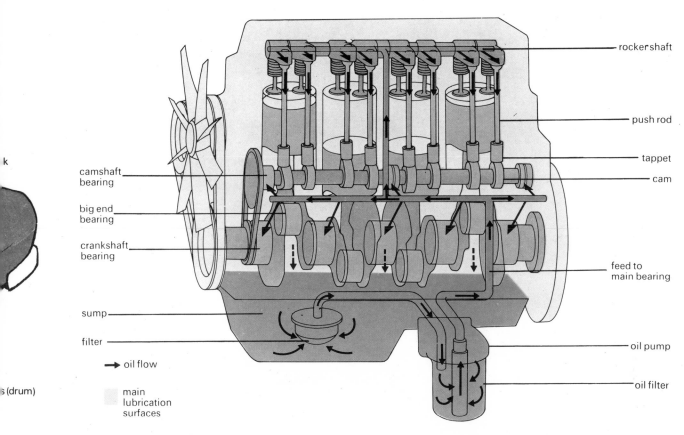

rocker shaft

push rod

tappet

cam

feed to
main bearing

camshaft
bearing

big end
bearing

crankshaft
bearing

sump

filter

oil pump

oil filter

→ oil flow

(drum)

main
lubrication
surfaces

It is connected, through the gearbox and driving-shaft, to the driving-wheels, which turn on the road surface and make the car go forward.

One easy way to remember the stages of the cycle is to learn the four words: suck, squeeze, bang, blow. The cylinder *sucks* in the petrol/air mixture, the piston moves up and *squeezes,* the spark makes a

bang which drives the piston down and *blows* out the burnt gas, or exhaust.

Most car engines have four cylinders which fire in turn, but six or even eight cylinders give more firings and so more power. Piston-engined aircraft engines may have thirty-six or more cylinders arranged in a circle.

Above Unless a flow of oil is kept moving between the working parts of an engine, they quickly wear out. As the engine turns, it works an oil pump which carries the oil round. On its way round the engine the oil picks up bits of dirt and tiny metal shavings. Some of these are filtered out, but all the oil must be drained out and a fresh supply put in every few thousand miles.

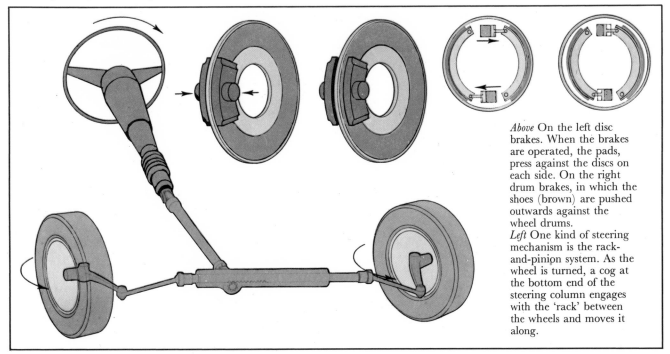

Above On the left disc brakes. When the brakes are operated, the pads, press against the discs on each side. On the right drum brakes, in which the shoes (brown) are pushed outwards against the wheel drums.
Left One kind of steering mechanism is the rack-and-pinion system. As the wheel is turned, a cog at the bottom end of the steering column engages with the 'rack' between the wheels and moves it along.

The Wankel engine

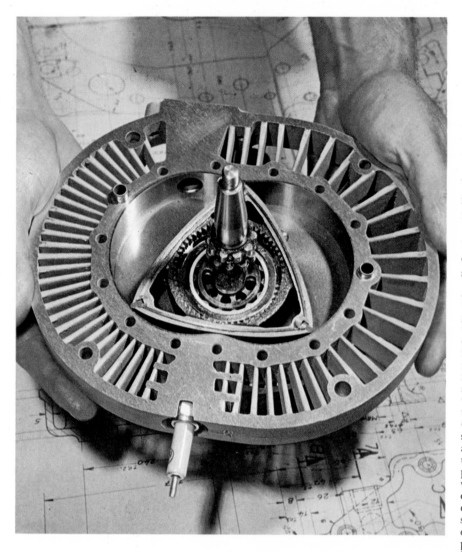

connected with the driving-shaft and the wheels in the usual way.

The Wankel engine is simpler than a piston engine and has fewer moving parts. Unfortunately, present-day Wankel engines leak too much fuel and gas between the vanes and the engine wall. As a result they use more fuel than piston engines to drive a car of similar weight the same distance.

Until the world oil crisis in 1973 the Wankel engine was becoming increasingly popular. But with petrol now many times dearer than it was before 1973, and with many scientists saying that the world has only another twenty or thirty years' oil left, the Wankel has suffered a set-back.

Left The cover has been removed from this Wankel engine to show the rotor. The gaps between the sides of the rotor and the inside wall of the engine are of different sizes. As the air and fuel mixture is swept past the sparking-plugs, the gap narrows and so the mixture is compressed ready to be fired by the spark. On the far side of the inside wall is the hole through which the exhaust gases escape.
the sequence: *suck, squeeze, bang, blow*.
Opposite A powerful V-8 piston engine, showing the internal working parts and also the 'extras' attached to it. As well as turning the driving-shaft, the crankshaft powers the cooling fan, the generator, which makes electricity for the lights and other equipment, the water pump, the distributor, which sends currents to the sparking-plugs, and the camshafts which open and close the valves to let in the petrol/air mixture. V-8 engines are usually fitted to large cars and give a very smooth ride.
Below The four-stage cycle of the Wankel engine. As in a piston engine, this follows

Although most engines have pistons which make an up-and-down movement inside their cylinders, there are other ways of producing power in an internal combustion engine. One of these is the rotary engine, usually called the Wankel engine after the name of its inventor.

The first Wankel engine was tried out in 1956, and it is now used in many thousands of cars. It wastes quite a lot of fuel, however, and until this problem has been solved it is unlikely to take over from the more usual piston engine.

Instead of pistons in cylinders the Wankel engine has a triangular rotor which revolves inside the engine wall. Each corner of the triangle is fitted with a vane–a flap of metal which is held by

springs against the engine wall. The vanes separate each gap from its neighbour.

As a vane passes the inlet port, the petrol and air mixture is drawn into the gap between rotor and engine wall. It is kept in that section by the next vane round. As the rotor moves on, the petrol and air mixture is compressed and brought round to the sparking-plug, which fires it. There is an explosion, just as in the piston engine, when the mixture is fired, and the expanding hot gases push the rotor round further. Now the exhaust gases can escape through the exhaust port, and meanwhile the whole cycle has started again with another gap drawing in fresh fuel and air. The Wankel engine's rotor is

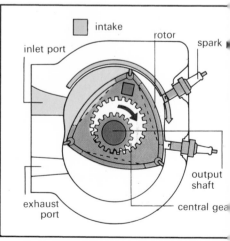

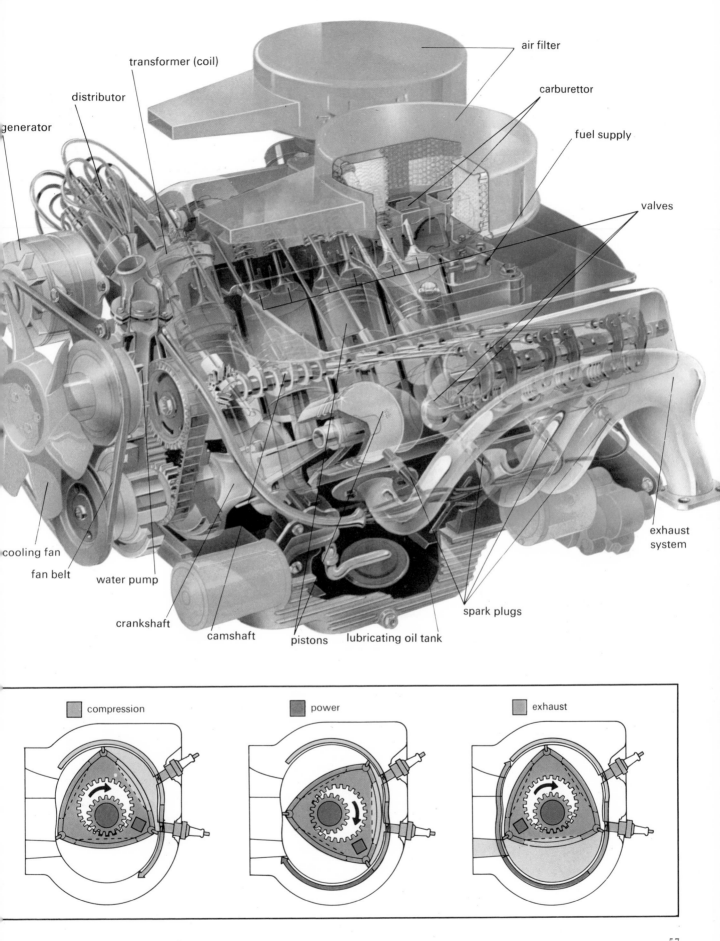

air filter

carburettor

fuel supply

transformer (coil)

distributor

generator

valves

cooling fan

fan belt

water pump

crankshaft

camshaft

pistons

lubricating oil tank

spark plugs

exhaust system

compression

power

exhaust

The motor cycle

Motor cycles are more manoeuvrable in traffic than cars and take up less parking space. Because they are much lighter than cars and carry only two people at most, they can accelerate faster and use less petrol. But they are the most dangerous vehicles on the roads. More motor-cyclists are killed or seriously injured each year than any other kind of road user. If you buy a motor cycle when you are older, make sure you learn to ride it properly and observe all the safety rules.

Motor cycles have petrol engines of many different types. Some have only one cylinder and piston, some two, three or four. Usually, the engine turns a crankshaft which is linked to the gearbox, and this in turn is connected with the rear wheel by a chain. But some machines have a drive-shaft like a car.

The engine is kept cool by the flow of air as the motor cycle goes along. The

Above A twin-cylinder four-stroke motor-cycle engine, with the cylinder arranged in a V-shape.

Below A powerful Honda 750 cc motor cycle with a four-cylinder engine. Part of the casing has been 'cut away' to show the arrangement of the gearbox and gear pedal. Like most motor cycles the Honda is chain-driven.

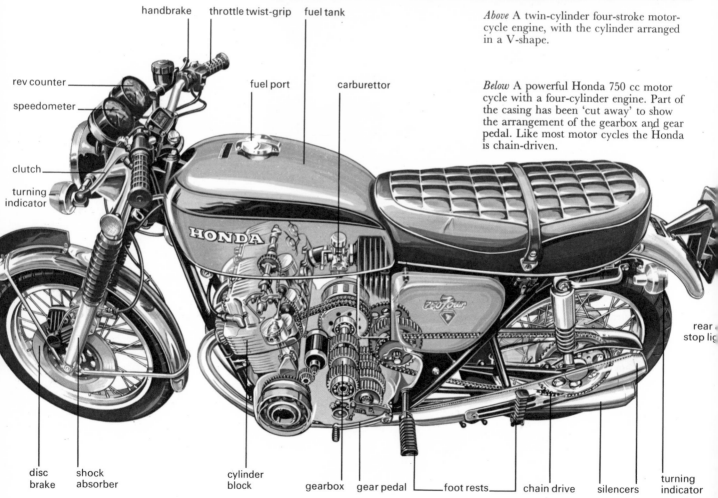

outside of the engine is vaned, so that a larger surface is exposed to the cooling air.

Like a cyclist, a motor-cyclist steers by turning the front wheel by means of handlebars. The handlebars also carry other controls–the clutch, which separates the crankshaft from the gearbox so that the rider can change gear, the front brake and the throttle, which controls the amount of fuel going into the engine. The motor-cyclist uses his feet to work the rear brake, to change gear and to start the engine.

The wheels of a motor cycle are connected to the body by powerful springs which absorb shocks from bumpy road surfaces. Without these the rider would be shaken to bits!

Many motor cycles have two-stroke engines. These are small and light, and although they don't develop much power, they are cheap to run and are used for 'runabout' machines.

In a two-stroke engine the piston goes through the cycle of *suck, squeeze, bang* and *blow* in one up-and-down movement. As it moves down the cylinder it

Above right A motor-cyclist cornering at speed. If he leans over too far, his tyres will lose their grip on the road and he will go into a skid.

Right Many motor-cyclists at one time fitted side-cars to take their wives or children. Side-cars are very rarely seen on the roads today, but they are still popular in motor-cycling sport. The side-car passenger in this picture is leaning inwards to stop the machine spinning off the track.

Right A 'snow scooter' fitted with a motor-cycle engine–and skis. It is used to travel across the frozen wastes of northern Canada–and it can carry passengers, too!

draws in the petrol and air mixture. Then it moves up, compressing the mixture. At the top of the stroke a spark ignites the mixture, and the piston is pushed down, driving the crankshaft round. At the same time the exhaust gases escape through a hole in the side of the cylinder. Two-stroke engines are also used in outboard motors for small boats, and in motor mowers.

Because there are only two wheels, riding a motor cycle calls for more skill and care than driving a car. The rider must judge his speed carefully and change gear at the right time. Cornering, too, needs great care. You will have seen a motor-cyclist leaning inwards as he goes round a bend like the rider in the picture at the top of this page. Unless he does this, the circular movement will push him outwards so that he either overbalances or ends up on the wrong side of the road. He must take care not to lean inwards too far, however; if he does, his rear wheel will slide sideways and throw him into a skid.

Skilled motor-cycling is very exciting to watch. The best place to see it is at a speedway track, a grass-track meeting or on a special moto-cross course, where riders use bikes specially adapted for split-second, high-speed work.

Yamaha motor cycles taking part in an obstacle race at a scramble meeting in the United States. Motor-cycle scramblers enjoy testing their machines against gruelling courses in hilly areas, or showing off their skills on a prepared track in a stadium. In Britain and America the sport is called 'scrambling'. In Europe they call it Moto-Cross.

Gears

Gears are used in most machinery. They can do two different jobs, sometimes at the same time. First, they can increase the amount of work that a source of energy can do; second, they can change the direction of the work.

Bicycle gears make it easier to cycle up hills. Riding on the level, the cyclist uses top gear. When he comes to a hill, he needs to pedal really hard to keep the cycle going unless he 'changes down'. Changing to a lower gear makes the same amount of effort do more work.

Imagine that you have two gears which mesh with each other, one with ten teeth and the other with twenty. If you turn the smaller gear, it will go round once while the twenty-tooth gear has made only half a revolution. With an arrangement like this you would be able to lift a heavy weight with a fairly small amount of effort. But if you turn the larger gear, it will go round once while the ten-tooth gear has done two revolutions. You would use this arrangement if you wanted more speed for your effort. The gear ratio—the proportion of teeth on one gear to those on the other—alters the performance of a set of gears.

In cycle gears your feet move round on the pedals in the same direction as the wheels on the road. There is no need to change the direction of your effort. In a car things are different. In most engines the crankshaft revolves end-on to the car's direction of travel. So the work done by the engine has to change direction in order to turn the driving-wheels. The direction is changed by having two gears which are set at right angles.

A similar change of direction can be seen in a rotary egg-whisk. The handle that you turn is connected to a gear which is set at right angles to the gear on the spindle of the whisk. This changes your vertical turning movement into the

Right In this machine the smaller wheel—the pinion—has only a quarter as many teeth as the larger, so it will turn four times as fast. The left-hand machine will lift the heavier weight. When the positions are reversed, only a smaller weight can be lifted, but at greater speed.

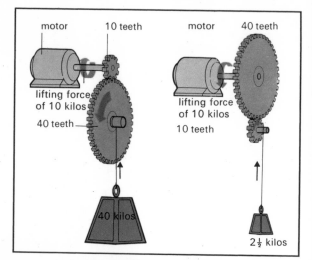

motor   10 teeth   motor   40 teeth

lifting force of 10 kilos   lifting force of 10 kilos

40 teeth   10 teeth

40 kilos   2½ kilos

Far left A set of bevel gears with tapered teeth. *Left* Helical gears with curved teeth used to transfer effort from one shaft to another parallel one. Helical and bevel gears with curved teeth work more quietly and with less wear than those with straight teeth, and are often used in machinery where noise must be kept down.

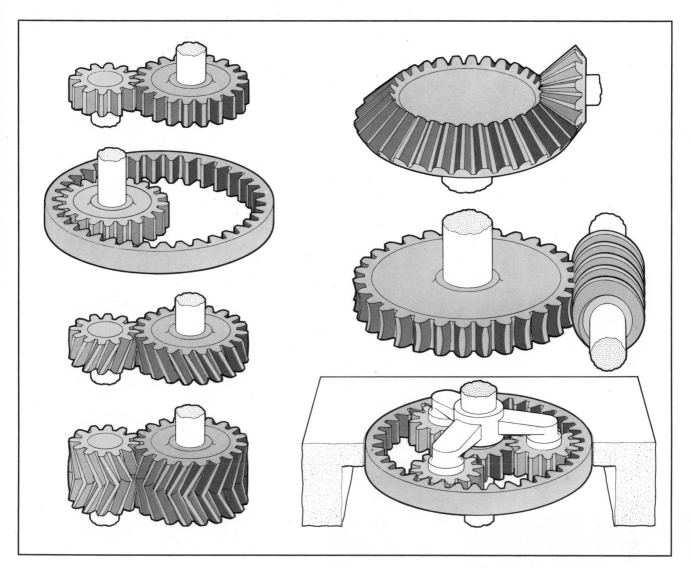

horizontal movement of the whisk as it beats the egg.

The best way to understand gears is to watch as many different examples as possible at work. Several different kinds are shown on these pages. If you keep your eyes open, you will find many more real-life examples all round you. And if you can get hold of an old clock, watch or clockwork motor you will be able to see exactly how gears work, turning the force that is applied to them into the work that we want them to do.

Right In an ordinary cycle without special gears the small gear on the rear wheel turns faster than the large gear on the pedal wheel. The chain enables the cyclist to pedal in the same direction as the wheels move. If the pedal gear were connected directly to the rear wheel gear, he would have to pedal backwards to cycle forwards! The small diagram to the left of the cycle shows why.

Above Seven different types of gear. In the left-hand column, from the top, first comes a spur gear, used, like the helical gear on the opposite page, to drive a parallel shaft. Next, an internal gear, in which both the pinion and the gear turn in the same direction. The helical gear has curved teeth to reduce noise. The gear with V-shaped teeth is a herring-bone type, making up a double helical gear.

Top in the right-hand column is a bevel gear, which changes the direction of the effort. The worm gear is another way of changing the direction. Here the teeth of the pinion form a continuous line, like the thread of a screw. At the bottom, a planetary gear system. The pinions turn on a central gear and on the internal ring gear. This system is used in cars with automatic transmissions.

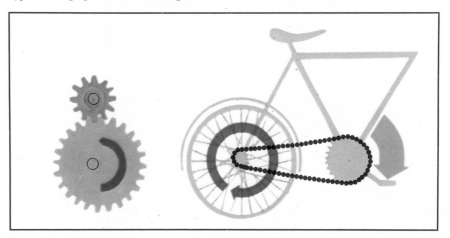

Elevators and escalators

There are two ways of moving people vertically inside a building. Lifts or elevators can take only a limited number of people at a time but they can be fitted into a small space such as the well of a staircase. Escalators need more room but they can carry more people, and, as they run continuously, there is no waiting.

Escalators are more efficient than lifts for some purposes—for example, at a busy underground station in the rush-hour. If a large number of passengers get off a train, they may fill up several lifts. Some will have to wait until the lift has made two or three journeys before they find a place—or face a climb up several hundred stairs. But a similar number of people can step on an escalator straight away and be swept quickly to the top.

Below left A modern lift in a busy store in Australia. One advantage of this glass-sided lift is that as they go from floor to floor passengers might see something they want to buy. The guide rails can be seen on each side of the lift carriage, but the counterweight is hidden by panelling. *Below* The working of a modern lift, showing the carriage and counterweight. A 'sheave' is the grooved pulley wheel, and this kind of lift mechanism is called a sheave system.

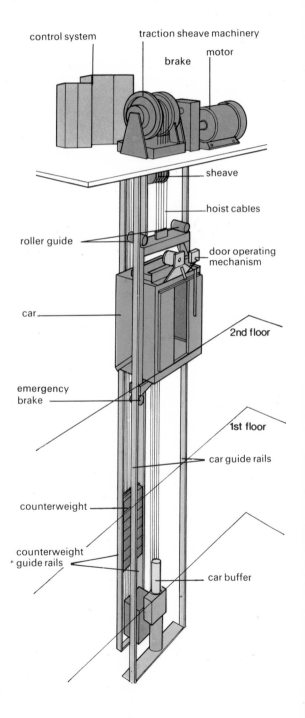

control system

traction sheave machinery

brake

motor

sheave

hoist cables

roller guide

door operating mechanism

car

2nd floor

emergency brake

1st floor

car guide rails

counterweight

counterweight guide rails

car buffer

Lifts have been used for miners and for carrying goods for many years. But until about 130 years ago no one went in a lift if they could avoid it. They were afraid that the rope would break. What changed all this was the invention of an American, Elisha G. Otis.

Otis's idea was a safety-catch which would operate if the rope broke. His lift ran between guide rails, which gave it a steadier ride. When he demonstrated his lift for the first time, Otis used a lift carriage with an open top so that he could reach the rope. As the lift went up, he reached up and cut the rope with a knife. People screamed and gasped – but at once powerful metal clamps grabbed the guide rails and held the lift in place. Passenger lifts have been fitted with safety brakes ever since.

The cables fixed to the top of the lift carriage go up to a wheel at the top of the shaft. The wheel is connected to a motor. Then the cables pass over the wheel and hang down the other side, where they are joined to a heavy weight which is called the counterweight. More cables go from the bottom of the carriage to the bottom of the counterweight, making an endless loop.

The counterweight balances the weight of the lift. When the lift carriage is going down, the counterweight goes up. This does some of the work of the motor and it also presses the cables against the pully to prevent slipping.

There are other safety devices in a lift besides Otis's safety brake. The carriage won't move unless the doors are closed properly, and the doors cannot be opened unless the carriage has stopped properly at a floor. If too many people get into the carriage, the motor shuts off and an alarm is sounded.

Modern lifts have complicated electrical controls, with lighted panels at each stop to show people exactly where the carriage is at the moment, and whether it's going up or down. Some of these control systems even have 'memories' so that when they have finished one journey they automatically move to the right floor to start the next. In very tall buildings there are 'express' lifts which zoom quickly up the lower floors and stop only at the higher ones. And inside the lift carriage there is an alarm button which passengers can press if anything goes wrong.

Escalators are moving staircases. They are built in pairs because, unlike

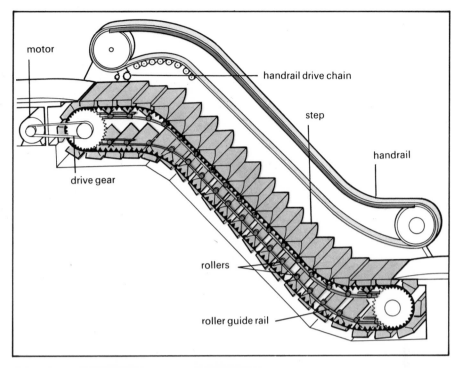

Above How an escalator works. The motor turns the top gearwheel, which meshes with the links of a continuous chain on which the steps are mounted. Each step has rollers to keep it level.

Left The escalator's younger brother, a travelator. Here there are no steps. The slope is continuous. A travelator is easier to use, especially for people with heavy luggage.

lifts, each escalator can take people only one way.

The steps that make up an escalator are joined together in an endless belt. The belt passes round rollers which are arranged so that at the top and bottom of the staircase the steps gradually level out. At the bottom the steps run flat for a metre or two so that people can easily get on and get their balance before the steps form themselves. At the top the steps flatten out again so that it is easy to step off. Then the steps disappear and stay flat for the downward journey. If the escalator is going down, then the 'hidden' steps travel upwards.

An escalator also has a handrail which is driven by the same motor as the staircase and moves at the same speed.

Between 5,000 and 8,000 people per hour can be carried by an escalator, depending on its speed. But escalators

are sometimes frightening for children and old people, and difficult for people carrying heavy luggage. One answer to these problems which is being introduced into airports and other busy places is the travelator, or moving pavement. This works in a similar way to an escalator, but the surface is a gradual slope instead of stepped. The endless belt in a travelator, or moving pavement, is made of heavy rubber which moves round rollers at each end of the ride. Travelators are comfortable to use only if the slope is a gradual one; for this reason they need a lot of space.

It would not be safe to let people step sideways off escalators or travelators, so in a building with several floors they are arranged in banks with one separate ride for each journey between floors. Space can be saved by arranging the escalators one above the other.

The telephone

When you make a telephone call, you are using the first method that man discovered of turning sounds into electrical signals and back again. Alexander Graham Bell, an American, made the discovery over 100 years ago, and our telephones today are very much the same as the one he invented.

The mouthpiece–the part you

signals from your voice–make the diaphragm move, and this movement makes the sound-waves that your friend hears.

When telephones were first invented, a caller had to ring the exchange and ask an operator to be connected to the line of the person he wanted to talk to. Then the operator would 'plug him in'

of connecting people automatically without talking to an operator was an American undertaker. Almon B. Strowger was sure that the operators at his local exchange were connecting callers with other undertakers in the town and so robbing him of business. If callers could get in touch with him direct, he thought, his business would improve. In 1889 he came up with the answer–the 'Strowger switch' automatic exchange, which is still in use in Britain and many other parts of the world. The diagram on the opposite page shows how it works.

It takes several seconds for a Strowger system to connect a caller with his number. When you dial, you can often hear the clicks as the system works out the number you are calling. While all this is going on, someone else may be trying to call you and getting an 'engaged' signal. So faster ways of finding and connecting numbers have been invented, using transistors–tiny crystals–instead of the clumsy Strowger switches.

Ways of connecting people on the telephone are being speeded up, but the telephone itself is still very much the same instrument that Alexander Graham Bell invented more than a century ago.

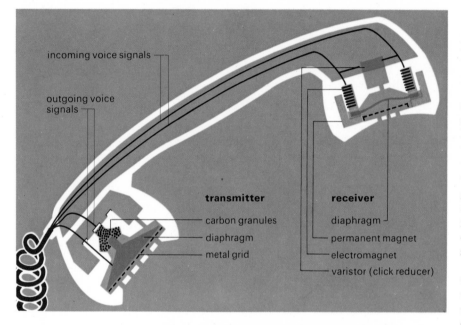

incoming voice signals

outgoing voice signals

transmitter
— carbon granules
— diaphragm
— metal grid

receiver
diaphragm
permanent magnet
electromagnet
varistor (click reducer)

speak into–is a very simple kind of microphone. The ear-piece–the part you listen to–is a simple loudspeaker. Telephones have to be simple and tough, because people drop them or slam them down or move them about. Voices on the telephone sound only *roughly* like the real voices of the speakers.

Behind the metal grid in the mouthpiece of a telephone are granules–small pieces–of carbon which have a weak electric current going through them. When you speak, the sound-waves shake up the carbon granules and alter the electric current. This travels along the telephone lines to the exchange, where it is connected to the line of the friend to whom you are speaking. Arriving at the ear-piece of your friend's telephone, the current travels in a coil round a magnet. The coil is connected with a diaphragm–a thin cone of metal or foil which can move to and fro. The alterations in the current–the electric

Above The plastic case of a modern telephone handset looks up to date, but the mouthpiece and ear-piece are still almost as simple as when Alexander Graham Bell invented the telephone over 100 years ago. The carbon granules in the mouthpiece cut out some of the sound-waves of the human voice, and this is why your friend's voice on the telephone may sound quite different from his real voice. *Right* Part of a modern telephone exchange in which new types of switches, using transistors, replace the clumsy and bulky Strowger type.

by taking the wires from the caller's line and joining them up with the line of the other person. This worked well enough when there were only a few people with telephones. But when the number of people with telephones grew, it was necessary to find a way of connecting people up without going 'through the operator'. Today you can dial the number of the person you want to talk to even if he lives across the other side of the world.

The first man to work out a way

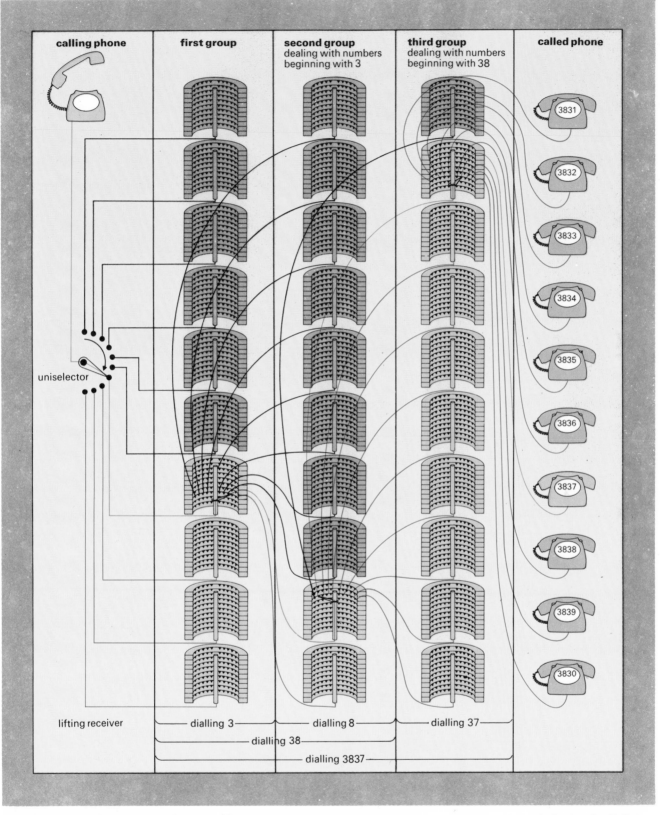

calling phone

first group

second group
dealing with numbers beginning with 3

third group
dealing with numbers beginning with 38

called phone

uniselector

3831
3832
3833
3834
3835
3836
3837
3838
3839
3830

lifting receiver — dialling 3 — — dialling 8 — — dialling 37 —

— dialling 38 —

— dialling 3837 —

Above How a Strowger switch system works. When the caller dials 3, he is connected to the selector that deals with all numbers beginning with 3. When he dials 8, the second group selector connects him with the selector that deals with numbers beginning with 38. And so on

when he dials 3 and 7. If there is no line free at any stage, he hears the 'engaged' signal. If all is clear, line 3837 gives a ringing tone and the subscriber answers.

The Strowger system is mechanical, and this makes it slow. Modern electronic systems using transistors can speed the

process up. A 'marker' takes the dialled number and searches through the lines to find out if it is possible to make a connection. If so, the call goes through. If not, the 'marker' can throw a switch which operates a recorded message telling the caller to try again later.

Radio

Radio-waves travel at the same speed as light-waves – at about 300,000 kilometres per second. If you could see them, they would be a similar shape to waves in the sea. They are made up of bursts of electric current, but the current is much less strong than the electricity going through the wires in your house, because radio-waves travel long distances and spread out as they go.

The sounds that you hear from your radio have come a long way in a short time. When America's moon explorers were speaking to Earth from the surface of the moon, their voices took only about seven-tenths of a second to travel the distance of about 385,000 kilometres!

The sound of a radio broadcast starts its journey at the microphone. This has a small electric current passing through it, and there is a grille at one end

Above A 'ribbon' microphone of the type often used in broadcasting studios. Behind the grille is a piece of metal ribbon hanging between the poles of a magnet. Sounds going into the microphone make the ribbon vibrate, and this makes changes in the electric current passing through the magnet. The current and the changes travel along wires to the transmitter.
Right How a sound travels to a radio transmitter through the air to a radio and a loudspeaker to the listener. A 'tuner' is the part of a radio set or a hi-fi which picks out the programme the listener wants and amplifies the signal before passing it on to the loudspeaker.

through which the sound of speech or music can pass. The sound changes the movements of the electric current only slightly if the sound is a quiet one but much more if it is loud.

Most transmitters from which radio-waves are sent out 'on the air' are some distance away from the studios from which the programmes are broadcast. The weak signals from the microphone are amplified, or made stronger, before being sent on to the transmitter. When they reach the transmitter, they are amplified again to make a good, strong signal which can be sent out.

Like the microphone the wires of a transmitter – which may be at the top of a tower or spread out across the ground – already have an electric current going through them. This is sending out radio-waves, but there is no

sound on them yet. When the sound signal is added to the radio-waves, it alters their shape. This is called 'modulation'.

It is quite easy to understand this if you imagine dropping a pebble into a pond. From the point where the pebble meets the water waves will spread out in circles. These waves are like the 'unmodulated' or 'carrier' signal out by the radio transmitter. If you now drop a second pebble at the same spot before the waves of the first pebble have died away, the second set of waves will mingle with the first and make them more choppy. The second set of waves is like the modulation made by the sound signals in the transmitter.

The modulated radio-waves spread out from the transmitter. Sometimes they spread all round, and sometimes – if the radio programme is broadcast from America for listeners in Europe, for example – they are beamed in one particular direction.

Because they spread out and have a long way to go, the signals become weaker as they travel. When they reach your radio, they must be made stronger again by being amplified. Your radio must also sort out the modulations made by the sounds from the transmitter's carrier wave.

Now the radio programme's journey is nearly over. Inside the radio the electric currents that make up the sound signal go to the loudspeaker, where they travel on a coil of wire round a magnet. Round the coil there is a diaphragm – a cone, usually made of thick paper. The currents in the coil move it to and fro slightly as they meet the lines of mag-

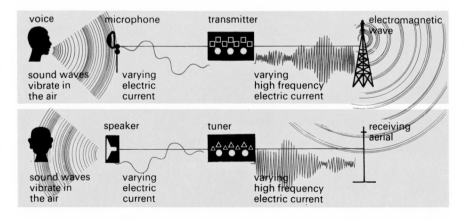

netism from the loudspeaker's magnet, and the cone turns these movements into sound. The sound-waves that come out of the loudspeaker are the same shape as those that went into the microphone, and so you are able to hear something that may be happening thousands of miles away.

Just like waves on the sea, radio-waves can be of any length. This is just as well, because if all radio-waves were the same length we could have only one radio programme to listen to! Transmitters send out waves of different lengths so that one programme doesn't get mixed up with another. When you turn the

Right Each radio station sends out a carrier (unmodulated) wave. Sounds to be transmitted alter (modulate) the carrier wave either in frequency (speed) or amplitude (waviness). *Below* The 177-metre Post Office Tower in London. Towards the top of the tower radio aerials send out signals for radio and TV networks, radio-telephone links and weather information.

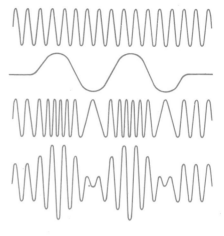

carrier wave unmodulated

modulating signal

frequency-modulated wave

amplitude-modulated wave

knob of your radio to find one particular station, the radio will pick up only the wavelength that you want to hear. Whenever you turn to that particular spot on the dial, you will always hear the same station. Most radio dials are marked with the names of stations or programmes to help you find them easily.

Waves behave differently according to their length. Long and medium waves, between about 10,000 and 100 metres long, travel close to the earth and can be easily picked up by radio sets–but because they are so close to the earth they are easily altered by other waves they may meet in the air. This is why you may hear 'interference' when you are listening to the radio on long or medium waves. Short waves travel upwards until they meet a layer round the earth which is called the ionosphere. This is about 250 kilometres up and is made up of small particles which bounce short radio-waves back to Earth again. Short waves are used for broadcasts over long distances. Finally, there are very short waves which are not bounced back by the ionosphere. These can be used only for local programmes.

On a radio set there is a switch which picks out the different 'wavebands' or sets of radio-waves used by the various radio stations. They are usually marked SW (for short wave), MW (for medium wave), LW (for long wave) and VHF or FM for very short wave. Cheap radios sometimes have only long and medium wavebands, but the sound quality may not be as good.

As well as programmes radio transmitters also send out messages between ships, aircraft, police cars, ambulances, fire appliances and even radio taxis. These services use short- or very short-wave transmitters.

Sound recording

One day in 1877 the American inventor Thomas Edison called his assistant into his office. Together they listened while Edison turned the handle of a machine on his desk. As he turned, they heard a voice reciting the nursery rhyme *Mary had a little lamb*.

It was the first time in the history of the world that sound had been recorded. What Edison had done was to speak into a horn which was connected with a needle playing over a tinfoil cylinder. The sound-waves from Edison's voice caused the needle to make tiny movements on the tin foil. When the tin-foil 'record' was played back, the sound-waves came back out of the horn.

Sound recording has come a long way since then, but it was Thomas Edison who started it.

Nowadays sound-waves are changed into electrical signals when a recording is made. Using a microphone, the waves become bursts of electricity which can be 'stored' in one of two ways.

One way is to put the signals on to tape. Recording tape is made of plastic,

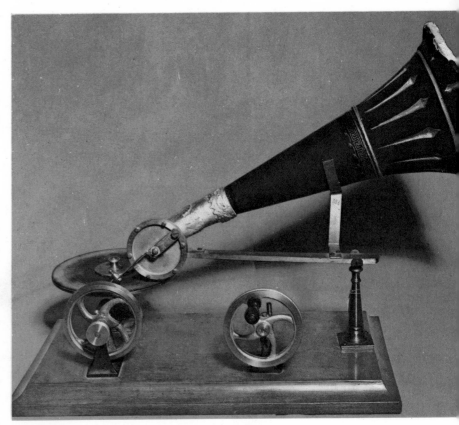

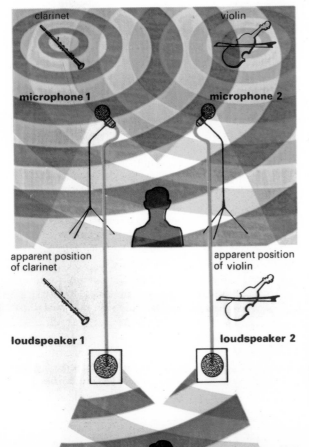

Above An early phonograph, as record-players were called. No electricity was used. The sound travelled from the needle to the small round end of the horn, called the 'sound-box'. Then it came out of the horn.

Left How stereo recording works. The blue bands are the sound-waves from the clarinet, and the yellow bands the sound-waves from the violin. Stereo recording keeps the waves separate so the listener hears them separately.

coated on one side–the dull side–with small particles of metal. When electrical signals come near it, the particles arrange themselves in patterns in much the same way as iron filings placed near a magnet. The patterns stay in position, and if the tape is played through a playback machine, the arrangements of particles make signals which can be turned back into sound-waves using a loudspeaker as in a radio.

When recordings are made in a studio, they are always made on tape, even if they will later be issued on discs. Tape-recording machines are smaller

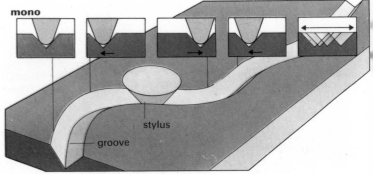

and easier to handle, and the tape can be edited–cut and joined again–so that bad notes or sounds that are not wanted–like coughs from the audience at a public concert–can be taken out. At the same time other sounds can be mixed in. When pop recordings are made, the backing–the instrumental music–is often recorded beforehand, and the singer performs to this recording. That way it's easier to go through the song again if the singer makes a mistake.

Stereo recordings are made by using two microphones–or two sets of microphones if a large orchestra is being recorded–and 'feeding' the signals to two separate tracks on the tape. When the tape is played back, each set of signals is changed back into soundwaves through different loudspeakers.

Most records played at home, however, are discs. The first stage in making a disc record is to cut a master disc from the original tape recording. This is done with a machine rather like a very heavy-duty record-player. A disc of metal is put on the turntable. A recording head–a heavy pick-up with a sharp cutting needle–is put on the disc. The signals from the original recording make a pattern of ripples and grooves on the metal disc. The disc is then used to make a mould from which the record you buy in the shop is pressed. When you play the record, the stylus in your pick-up turns the signals from the ripples and grooves back into sounds once more.

Stereo recordings give a very 'life-like' effect, but the latest development in sound recording is 'quadraphonic sound', in which recordings are made–and played back–from four sets of microphones. This may be the method of the future.

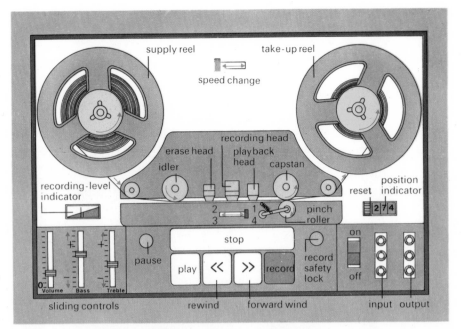

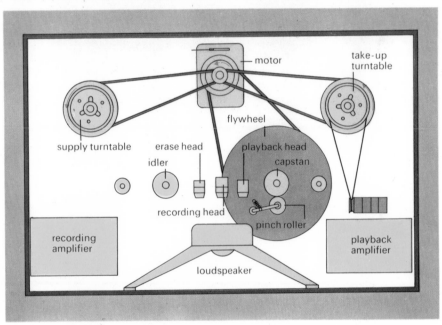

Below and left When a mono disc is cut, the cutter moves from side to side, making the ripples in the disc. On a stereo disc the cutter moves up and down as well as from side to side, so that two sets of signals can be recorded.

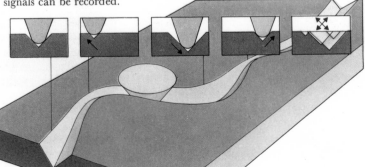

stereo

Above The top diagram shows the controls of a tape-recorder. The sliders on the left control the loudness and quality of the recording. The buttons in the middle allow the tape to be fast-wound backwards or forwards. The tape moves from the left-hand to the right-hand reel past the heads. The recording head transfers electrical signals to the tape. When a tape is played back, the playback head picks up the signals and turns them into an electrical current. The erase head enables tape to be used over and over again by cleaning off earlier recordings.

The bottom diagram shows what is beneath the controls. There are separate amplifiers for recording and playback and a motor to drive the tape reels. The pinch roller presses the tape close to the heads to ensure good recording or playback. The capstan– the large wheel that drives the tape–is kept going at an even speed by the large, heavy flywheel.

Television

Just as sound-waves can be turned into electrical signals which travel through the air to make radio programmes, light-waves, too, can be transmitted in much the same way. When you watch television, your TV set collects signals through its aerial and turns them back into light and sound.

Television pictures start with the camera in the studio. In the diagram below the camera is pointing at an apple. It must pick up the light part of the apple, where the skin is reflecting the studio lights, and the darker parts round the edge where the apple is shaded. It must also pick up the greens and reds on the skin.

If you took a colour photograph, the film would pick up all this information at the same time. A TV camera works differently. Like an ordinary camera it has a lens at the front – but that is about the only way in which the two are alike.

Behind the TV lens is a layer of material sensitive to light. The TV camera 'shoots' an electric current at this layer, moving up and down and across the picture at the rate of twenty-five complete pictures each second. As the current strikes each tiny part of the picture – there are 200,000 of them – it is altered by the amount of light in that part. So as the current moves over the picture, it copies it in the form of electrical signals.

So far the camera has only picked up light and dark parts of the picture. What about colour?

You will have learned from painting that all colours are mixtures of the primary colours. The primary colours for painting are blue, yellow and red. For colour TV they are blue, *green* and red. In a colour TV camera there is a separate tube for each of these three colours. The blue tube will pick up only the blueness of different parts of the picture, the green tube only the greenness, and so on. If the camera is pointed at something purple, for example, the

red and blue tubes will pick up their own parts of the colour.

So the camera collects three separate sets of signals from each picture. These are then combined into one signal which goes to the TV transmitter, where it is turned into radio-waves. Because there is so much information to be sent out about a TV picture, wide bands of waves have to be used, and these are called 'channels'.

When the waves arrive at your set, they have to be turned back into light. The screen of the set is the big end of a tube, and the back of the screen is coated with chemicals sensitive to light-waves of the three primary colours. As in the camera, there is a 'gun' which 'shoots' electric currents at the screen. In a colour set there are three separate guns, each dealing with the currents concerning one of the primary colours. The guns move up and down and across the screen, and as they go the currents light up points of light. The currents

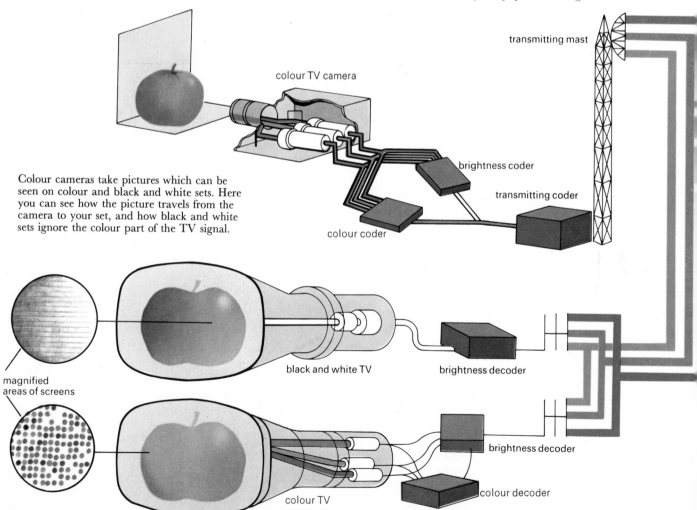

Colour cameras take pictures which can be seen on colour and black and white sets. Here you can see how the picture travels from the camera to your set, and how black and white sets ignore the colour part of the TV signal.

colour TV camera

transmitting mast

brightness coder

transmitting coder

colour coder

magnified areas of screens

black and white TV

brightness decoder

colour TV

brightness decoder

colour decoder

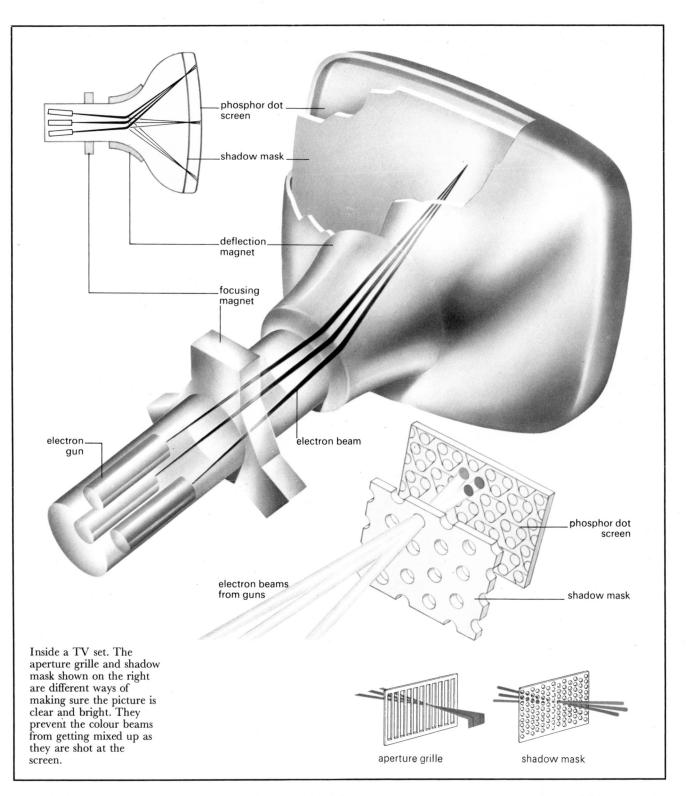

phosphor dot screen

shadow mask

deflection magnet

focusing magnet

electron gun

electron beam

electron beams from guns

phosphor dot screen

shadow mask

Inside a TV set. The aperture grille and shadow mask shown on the right are different ways of making sure the picture is clear and bright. They prevent the colour beams from getting mixed up as they are shot at the screen.

aperture grille

shadow mask

from the blue gun light up only the blue spots, and so on. In black and white sets there is only one gun and only one kind of dot on the screen.

We can all watch the same programmes, whether we have colour or black and white sets. A black and white set simply ignores the part of the TV signal which separates the colours and deals only with brightness and darkness.

Sound as well as the picture are needed to make a television programme. The sound is dealt with quite separately. It is collected by a microphone, just as in a radio programme, and sent out as radio-waves to be picked up by the radio part of the TV set. Because all radio-waves travel at the same speed, those which carry the signals of the sound arrive in your set at exactly the same moment as those which carry the picture.

How television works is a fascinating subject, and perhaps you will want to read about it in more detail. Possibly you could arrange to visit a TV station through your school or a club. But

whatever you do, *never* try to find out more about television by taking the back off a set. The working parts are dangerous.

Some television programmes are broadcast 'live'—what you see on the screen is actually happening at that moment, either in a studio or somewhere else like a football pitch or a sports stadium.

Other programmes are recorded. The sound and pictures have been turned into electrical signals and recorded on tape. Tape used for television is called video tape. It is wider than sound-recording tape because it has to carry more signals, but otherwise video recording is very similar to sound recording.

A third kind of programme is on film—either film made for the cinema or special TV film. The film is projected on to the lens of a camera and picked up in the same way as a live show.

Some programmes, especially news bulletins, are made up of live, taped and filmed parts, all put together so skilfully that you can't tell the difference.

Nearly all the plays and comedy shows on TV are made on tape or film. They can then be shown several times, either from the same TV station or in different parts of the world. The exchange of programmes between different countries allows us all to enjoy the performances of the world's best actors and musicians.

The floor of a TV drama studio, where the actors work, is lit brightly by lamps high in the roof above. The actors move about in sets—scenery built to look like the different places in which the action takes place. If the play shows a room, only two or three sides of it are built, leaving the rest open for the cameras to move in.

The cameras move about the floor silently on heavy trolleys with the cameraman sitting on board. As in an ordinary camera, there is a viewfinder through which the cameraman can see what he is 'shooting'. The camera trolley also carries a boom—a pole from which a microphone hangs. This can be moved so that it is as close as possible to the actors—but, of course, the cameraman must take care to keep the microphone out of the picture!

High on one wall of the studio is the gallery—a sound-proof room from which the play is directed. The director and his assistants can look out of the gallery window to see what is going on below—but most of the time they look at a set of TV screens mounted on their desk. The screens show what is being

Right A TV film unit filming a fire for a news programme. The man with the headphones is recording the sound.

Below TV is used in factories as well as for programmes at home. Here the screens show what is happening at different stages of steel-making. The picture can give a warning if anything goes wrong.

picked up by the various cameras on the floor. By pressing a switch the director can move the action from one camera to another. For example, the actors might walk out of one room into another. One camera will be set up to 'shoot' them as they go out of the door, and another will face the door of the room they are entering. At exactly the right moment the director switches from the first camera to the second without any break in the picture.

The director can speak through a microphone to the cameramen, who all wear headphones. In this way he can tell the cameramen to move closer to the actors or swing their cameras slowly round the set to catch some new piece of action. If something goes wrong, he can tell the cameramen and actors to stop so that the scene can be tried again.

The camera

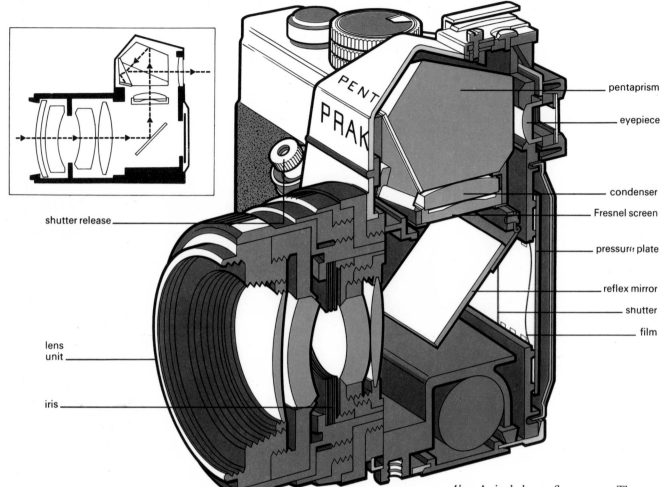

shutter release

lens unit

iris

pentaprism

eyepiece

condenser

Fresnel screen

pressure plate

reflex mirror

shutter

film

Cameras work by focusing the light rays from the scene in front of the lens on to a piece of light-sensitive film. The scene is 'stored' until the film is taken out of the camera, developed and printed.

The camera lens can 'see' only what is put in front of it. No matter how much a camera costs, it is the skill of the photographer that makes a good picture.

The camera case must be completely light-proof except through the lens, and a shutter prevents light from coming in that way except when a picture is being taken. In simple cameras the lens is fixed and will take fairly good pictures on objects at any distance. In more expensive cameras the lens can be moved to and fro to bring the object into sharp focus. Special lenses may also be fitted. A telephoto lens gives a close-up view of a distant object. A wide-angle lens gives a wide view, perhaps of a stretch of countryside. 'Fish-eye' lenses take

a picture of a whole semicircle – 180 degrees – in front of the camera. The first cameras used glass plates coated with chemicals. These plates were about the size of a page of this book, and you can imagine how large the early cameras had to be. In those days taking photographs was a fiddly business. The photographer had to work under a thick black cloth, and when he changed the plates he had to make sure no light reached them. Nowadays things are much easier.

Each photograph is taken on a separate length of film, which must be wound on before another picture is taken. Some cameras have a safety-catch to prevent a second picture being taken until the film has been wound on. When the whole film has been used, it is taken out of the camera and is ready for developing. Until it is developed all light must be kept away from the film surface, and in most cameras these days

Above A single-lens reflex camera. The mirror, Fresnel screen and pentaprism enable the photographer to see exactly what scene he will get on the picture. The small diagram shows how this works. Some cameras have separate viewfinders with their own lenses. These give a less accurate idea of how the picture will look. *Below* The stages in the developing and printing of black and white film.

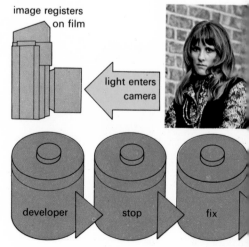

image registers on film

light enters camera

developer   stop   fix

the used film is safely wound up inside a plastic or metal can.

The chemical coating on the lens side of the film has been changed by the light that came in through the lens when the picture was taken. But this change cannot be seen yet. When the film is put into a dish of chemical developer, the shapes and lines of the image in the photograph begin to show up. For photographers who do their own developing this is one of the most interesting and exciting moments.

Because the film is still sensitive to light, developing is done in darkness or in dark red light. When the picture has been developed enough, it is 'fixed' by putting it into a bath of another chemical. If this were not done, the picture would go on developing until it was completely spoiled.

On the film now is a negative of the original scene. A white face will be black, and a black dog will come out white. The greys cannot be seen very clearly at all. A positive print is now made from the negative. Light is shone through the negative on to printing paper, which is sensitive to light like the original film. Where the negative is dark, the light cannot get through, and so the paper under these areas stays white. Light passing through the lighter parts of the negative turns the paper dark. In this way the blacks and whites are reversed.

A negative placed straight on to the printing paper will make a positive of the same size, and this is called a contact print. Larger prints – enlargements – are made by putting the negative into an enlarger, a machine which works like a slide projector. A strong light shines through the negative and a lens under-

neath on to the paper. The lens makes the picture larger, and by moving it closer to or further from the printing paper the photographer can choose a small or a large print.

Prints, like negatives, must be developed and fixed, using the same chemicals as before.

Developing and printing black and white film can quite easily be done at home, provided a room can be blacked out and there is somewhere safe to keep the chemicals. Colour film, however, is more difficult to develop, and most people have their colour films developed and printed at special laboratories.

Colour film is really three films in one, each on top of the other. The top

Above This photograh was taken with a 'fish-eye' lens which focuses light rays from a very wide angle. But it distorts the view. The iron railings are really in a straight line, and the people to the left of the monument are not really as far away as they look.

layer is sensitive to blue light, the second layer to green, and the third to red. The layers are developed one at a time, and when all three are put together, the result is a picture in the colours of the original scene. This can either be made into a transparency for showing in a slide projector, or a print on paper can be made from it.

Any camera can take either colour or black and white pictures. It all depends on the kind of film used.

Some cameras can make prints as soon as the picture is taken without waiting for the film to be finished, taken out and developed. In the Polaroid camera the chemicals on the film surface are developed and fixed into a positive by a second chemical which is spread over the film when it is pulled out of the camera case. The camera manufacturers Kodak make another kind of 'instant' camera in which the positive is developed when it is exposed to the air. 'Instant' cameras are useful for family and holiday pictures but they are difficult to copy or enlarge. Both black and white and coloured pictures can be taken.

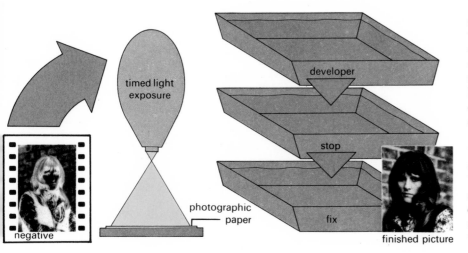

negative

timed light exposure

photographic paper

developer

stop

fix

finished picture

Infra-red photography

Everything in the world – even ice – radiates heat, just as everything radiates light. Heat and light both come to us from the sun and are 'bounced off' by objects around us.

We can feel the heat radiating from a sandy beach on a sunny day, but we can't feel the heat radiating from, say, a tree. However, it is possible to 'see' heat radiation by taking pictures of it using special film which is sensitive to infra-red rays. The pictures on these pages were taken in that way.

When you take an ordinary photograph, you 'capture' on the film the light rays bounced off the objects in the picture. If there is not enough light, you cannot take a good picture unless you use a flash bulb. Infra-red film can work in the dark, because it captures the heat rays from the objects in front of it.

Because infra-red film sees a different picture from the human eye, it can take pictures which tell us things we didn't know, or can't see, about the world around us.

The pictures on these pages show two examples of this.

The picture below is of a jet engine being tested. It shows the amount of heat being given off by each part of the engine. The hottest parts show up brightest. From this picture engineers can tell whether any part is getting too hot. Opposite is an infra-red picture of part of California. Different crops or trees radiate different amounts of heat and show up the patchwork pattern of the countryside.

The computer

Computers are machines that can do calculations very quickly. They can also store information in their 'memory banks' and bring it out again when it is needed. Computers worked out the calculations needed to send men to the moon. But they are also used in more everyday work. A computer works out your telephone bill.

Computers are not magic and they cannot think for themselves. They can do only what they are told to do, and they can only do it properly if they are given all the necessary information.

The set of instructions that tells a computer what to do is called the program. When you do a new kind of sum at school, you have to learn the rules for doing that particular sum. In the same way the program teaches the computer the rules for the work it has to do.

The program is made by a programmer. He works out how the computer can do its 'sums' step by step. He writes down these steps in a way that can be fed in to the computer, usually on cards or paper tape in which holes have been punched. The different position of the holes makes up the computer's 'language'.

The program may tell the computer how to work out the cost of your telephone bill by multiplying the number of units of telephone time you have used by the price per unit. Or the program may be about some much more difficult problem, like how to work out how strong an aircraft's wings have to be to stand up to the strain of flying at Mach 1. Unless the programmer does his work properly, you may get a telephone bill that is too big–or the aircraft's wings may fall off.

Left A computer programmer must work out each operation step by step. For this he uses a 'flow chart'. This flow chart is from a program instructing a computer how to index a book. Each step presents a yes-or-no choice.
Below Parts of a computer system which shows its results on a screen. The input information is processed by the program, and data is added from the back-up store. When all the work is done, the results are printed out on the screen.

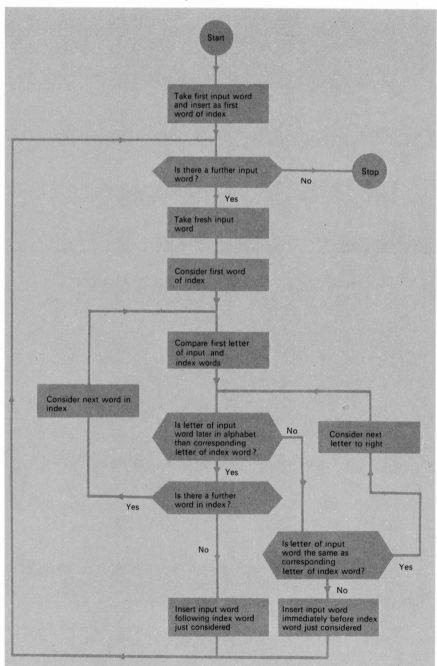

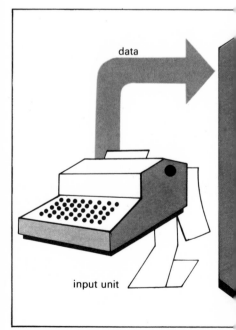

The program is stored in the computer's memory bank, together with the programs for other jobs that the computer might have to do. Also in the memory bank is the back-up store–information that is needed when the work starts. In the case of the telephone bill this will include your name and address, the account number, the number of your telephone and details of any money you owe from the last bill.

The next stage is for an operator to feed in the details on which the computer is to work–the figures of the sums. These are tapped out on a keyboard similar to a typewriter keyboard. The operator chooses the program, feeds in the details, and the computer gets to work, bringing in the information from the back-up store. In the case of the telephone bills the operator will also tell the computer what to do with the

Above The computer room in a Los Angeles bank. *Left* A computer print-out unit. The results can now be filed or posted, or checked by hand. The roll of paper in a print-out unit which sends out bills would be pre-printed with details of the company, how to pay and possibly other information.

data

results

output unit

back-up store

results. He presses a 'print' button, and the bills come out of the machine, addressed and ready for posting. But if it is only the answer to a sum that is required, this may be shown on a television screen. If the calculations might be needed again, they can all be stored away on recording tape for further use.

As computers work by electricity, they cannot use our alphabet of twenty-six letters or our decimal system of ten digits. An electrical circuit can be only either on or off. So a computer can understand only two words–yes (on) and no (off)–and two digits–1 (on) and 0 (off). The two-digit system is called the binary system, and each column in a binary sum represents 2 instead of 10 as in the decimal system. Five comes out as 101–one 4, no 2s, one 1. In the same way a computer can make only one choice of action at a time. It 'thinks' like someone walking round a maze. It tries each turning and comes back again if it meets a dead end. But it can work so quickly that this doesn't matter. And in spite of using the binary system, which means working in numbers hundreds of digits long, it can do in seconds calculations that would take a whole team of human beings several months to work out.

Perhaps best of all the computer can do a great deal of work that would be boring to people. It never gets bored and it never gets tired, and so it makes fewer mistakes.

The compass

The easiest way to find out how a compass works is to make one. You will need a needle, a cork, a small dish and a magnet.

First, magnetize the needle by stroking it, in one direction only, with the magnet. Keep stroking for about half a minute. Test the needle by seeing if it will pick up another needle or a metal paper-clip.

When you are satisfied that the needle has been magnetized, put it carefully through the cork so that an equal length of needle sticks out at each side.

Next, mark the points of the compass on the rim of the dish, using a felt pen or Indian ink. Put a spot of colour anywhere you like round the rim. Then take a ruler and lay it across the dish so that it crosses over the exact middle. Where the ruler meets the rim opposite your first mark make another. Lay the ruler across again, so that you divide the area of the dish into quarters, and make two more marks. The four dots should be equally spaced round the rim.

You could letter the four dots N for north, S for south (opposite N), W for west (to the left of N and S) and E for east (to the right). If it's difficult to put letters on the rim, you can 'read' the compass by making one of the dots a different colour. This will be north.

Put enough water in the dish to enable the cork to float, put the needle and cork in the water, and you should see it swing slowly round until it comes to rest in one position. This position is magnetic north. Carefully turn the dish so that the needle is pointing directly at your N dot.

Although your compass is a very simple one, it is very similar to the first compasses used by sailors in Europe about 1,000 years ago. They, too, used a bowl of water, but they put their magnets on a piece of wood or straw.

The reason why the needle swings to magnetic north is that the Earth itself is a huge magnet with a North Pole and a South Pole. The north poles of magnets attract each other, and the north pole of your needle is attracted by the Earth's North Pole.

Unfortunately, there is one thing that complicates the use of a compass. The Earth's magnetic north is not in the same position as true north. True north is in the middle of the top of the world, like the stalk on an apple. But magnetic north moves about. At the moment it is several hundred kilometres away from true north, off Victoria Island in northern Canada.

The difference between a compass reading and the direction of true north is called declination, and it varies from place to place. If you were using a compass to navigate, you would have to allow for declination, and you would have a chart that told you how much the declination was for the area you were in.

The main points of the compass that you marked on the rim of your home-made instrument are called the 'cardinal points'. In between them are other points. The point half-way between north and east is called north-east. The point between north-east and north is called north-north-east. And so on round the dial, making thirty-two points in all.

An easier way of making readings, however, is by numbers. The circle is divided into 360 degrees, starting with 0 at north. North-east can then be called north 45 degrees east, or the compass reading becomes a 'bearing' – a number between 1 and 359 which is the number of degrees between north and the compass needle.

Left A yacht compass. The two spheres on either side are magnets used to correct the 'declination'. The compass card is marked in both degrees and the points of the compass.

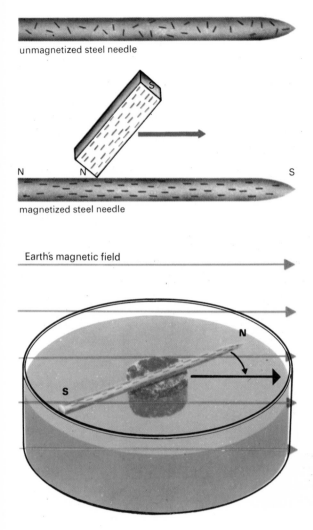

unmagnetized steel needle

magnetized steel needle

Earth's magnetic field

Left How to make your own compass. The action of stroking the needle with a magnet lines up the tiny 'magnets' in the steel, in the same way as the needle, when placed in the water, lines itself up with the Earth's magnetic field.

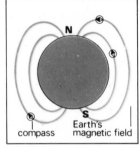

Above When a compass goes near one of the poles of the Earth, its needle dips, and this can be a cause of compass errors. The problem can be corrected by weighting the opposite end of the needle.

problems because of the aircraft's metal engines and batteries. If you put a piece of iron or steel near your home-made compass, you will find that the needle swings, and the reading is then inaccurate. Any electrical tool–a shaver, for example–placed near the compass will make the needle swing even more, even if the tool is switched off. You can imagine the effect on a compass of the equipment in an aircraft!

This problem is solved by shielding an aircraft's compass with magnets which compensate for, or cancel out, the magnetic fields round about. In addition the compass itself consists of a metal cylinder mounted vertically in an oil-bath. There is a window in the side of the oil-bath through which the compass bearings, marked on the side of the cylinder, can be read off.

Modern ships and aircraft do not rely on ordinary compasses for navigation, however. They use a special kind of compass called a gyrocompass, which is not magnetic and so is not affected by magnetic fields near it.

If you are using a compass on land, you have to hold it level and still while you take a reading. Ships, of course, can't stand still when they are at sea and they are always on the move, swinging and rolling as well as pushing through the water. To cope with this problem ships' compasses float in a glass bowl containing a liquid–often alcohol as this will not freeze in even the coldest weather. Even when the ship rolls, the surface of the liquid stays horizontal, and the compass continues to give accurate, steady readings.

On the outer case of a ship's compass is a black line called the 'lubber line' which points to the front of the ship. The point on the compass dial next to it shows the direction in which the ship is going. When the ship turns, the compass card, with the points and degrees marked on it, stays still, and the lubber line, moving with the ship, takes up a new position on the dial. The turn can then be measured in degrees.

Aircraft compasses present special

Right This map of the area surrounding the North Pole shows how declination–the angle between true north and magnetic north–varies from place to place. This angle has to be taken into account when a navigator is plotting his course using a compass. Another complication is that magnetic north is not fixed–it moves slowly from west to east of true north. You will often see on the edge of a map a mark showing true and magnetic north and the declination for the area shown on the map at the date the map was made.

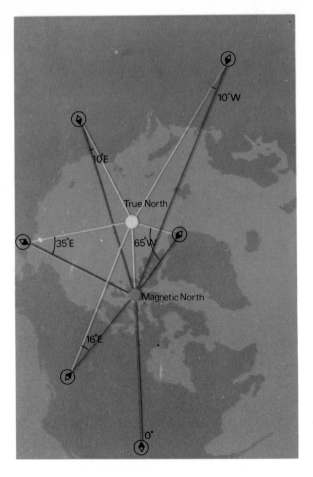

The laser beam

Like sound, electricity and every other form of energy, light travels in waves. Ordinary sunlight is made up of all the colours of the spectrum, and each colour has a different wavelength. Sunlight quickly spreads out in all directions. The different waves are out of step with each other, and this is why we can see some colours more easily than others at a distance. Red light contains mainly red waves, and these move in step with each other. Red is an easy colour to pick out, and for this reason it is used as a danger signal on railways and at traffic lights. But although the waves of red light keep in step, they do not stay parallel with each other.

If light is concentrated into a very narrow beam and made very bright by bouncing it to and fro between mirrors, it makes a source of energy so powerful that it can even cut a hole in a diamond, the hardest substance on Earth.

What happens in a laser is not hard to understand if you imagine rolling a 'sausage' of modelling clay in your hands. As you do this, the 'sausage' rolls out into a long, thin string. But imagine what would happen if the length of the clay were to stay the same because you had put some hard substance at each end to prevent it getting longer. If you were able to put enough pressure on the clay, it would be squeezed and become more and more condensed. At the end you would have a very dense, very tough length of clay, of sausage length but string thickness. It would be very strong indeed.

A laser takes light-waves and squeezes them up in a similar way. The first laser ever invented used red light, but other colours have been used since. Red light was chosen because its waves run in an orderly pattern.

The first laser used a rod of synthetic ruby packed into a glass tube. Synthetic ruby – made in a factory – was used

Above The first laser, built in 1960, used a rod of synthetic ruby which produced red laser light, but other materials have since been used. This is an argon gas laser, in which the flashlight passes through a container of gas giving off blue-green light. Because laser light is so powerful, workers using it have to wear protective clothing. This worker is safe behind a protective screen.

Right Sunlight is a mixture of colours of many different wavelengths, each moving in its own way. The waves are out of step, and this is why the edges of the colours in the spectrum of sunlight are fuzzy. Red light waves move in step, but they are not parallel. The spectrum of red light is also fuzzy at the edges. Red laser light waves are in step *and* parallel. The spectrum of red laser light is clear and sharp at the edges.

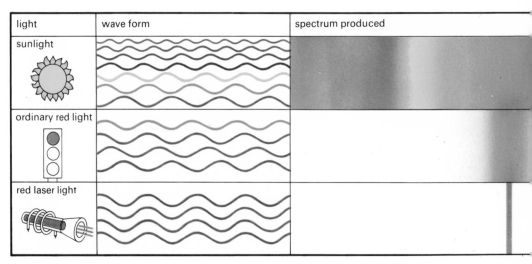

light	wave form	spectrum produced
sunlight		
ordinary red light		
red laser light		

instead of the natural stone because the atoms in it are arranged in the same way all through. Round the ruby rod was coiled a flash tube – an ordinary electric-light tube which could flash very brightly.

When the light flashed, it set off a chain of activity inside the ruby rod. The atoms began to rush about, sending out great waves of energy as they did so. At one end of the glass tube was an ordinary mirror. At the other was a mirror which allowed some light to pass through. As the atoms rushed about inside the ruby crystal – with the light flashing again and again to get them even more excited – they bounced backwards and forwards between the mirrors. Some of the weaker atoms fell away to the sides, but the stronger ones went on getting stronger as they flashed to and fro. As they moved faster, they began to travel alongside each other in parallel waves. At last these waves were so strong that they could pass through the mirror which would allow them through, and what came out was red laser light.

Because it has been squeezed and pressed into parallel waves, laser light has great strength. For the same reason it does not spread out as other light-waves do. It makes a pin-point of light similar to that of a pencil-torch but much stronger and narrower. When a laser beam was flashed from Earth to the moon, it spread out to only about three kilometres even after a 385,000 kilometre journey through space!

A magnifying glass can be used to concentrate the rays of the sun so that they burn through paper. Laser light is so powerful that it can burn through anything. But what makes it such an important discovery is that because it is concentrated into such a tiny pin-point it can be used for very precise, accurate work which no other cutting tool can do.

Laser light can be used to drill or cut or weld tiny parts of precision machinery. It can even be used in dentistry and surgery, where a tiny piece of decayed tooth or dead body tissue needs to be cut away.

Lasers were discovered as recently as 1960, and no doubt many more uses for them will be found in future.

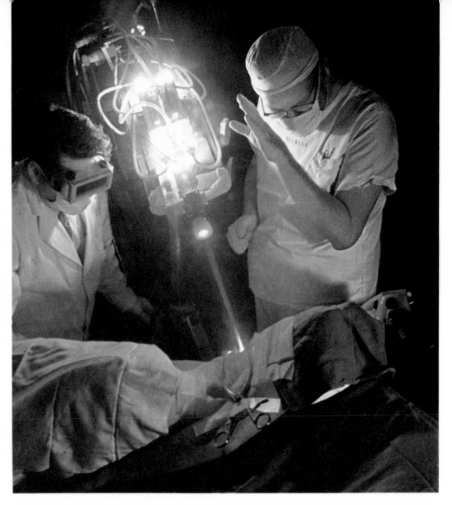

Above Lasers have proved valuable tools for the surgeon because they can be used with such great accuracy. Here surgeons are using a laser beam to treat skin cancer. Unless the cancerous tissue is removed, it will spread. Under a laser beam it absorbs the light and is destroyed by it. Healthy skin remains unharmed.

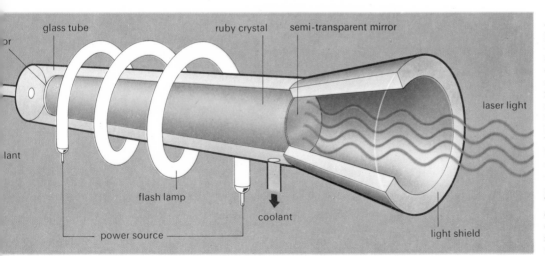

glass tube   ruby crystal   semi-transparent mirror

laser light

lant

flash lamp

coolant

power source

light shield

Left A model of the first ruby laser. When the lamp flashes, it excites activity among the ruby crystal's atoms. This activity builds up as the flashes continue, and a movement begins along the length of the crystal between the two mirrors. When this movement becomes strong enough, the energy passes through the semi-transparent mirror as red laser light. The heat that develops during this process is carried away by a cooling system in the same way as the heat of a car engine.

The microscope

What does a speck of dust really look like? What's inside a grain of salt? Is there anything in a drop of water as well as water?

We can't answer questions like these with our own eyes. The speck of dust, the grain of salt and the tiny organisms in water are too small. The instrument that can give us the answers is the microscope.

The microscope makes use of the way that lenses bend and focus rays of light. In a simple microscope there are just two lenses–the 'objective', which is close to the object being magnified, and another in the eyepiece. Scientists use compound microscopes, which have many more lenses. A good microscope can magnify an object up to 18,000 times–that is, make it look 18,000 times bigger than it really is. But when an object is magnified as much as this, it cannot be seen very clearly. Optical microscopes of the kind described on this page are used to magnify objects up to about 2,000 times. For greater magnifications an electron microscope, using electric currents instead of light, is used.

To look at an object under an optical microscope it must first be put on a slide. This is a 'sandwich' of glass which holds the object in position. Sometimes, if the object is to be seen clearly, it must be stained with a dye to make the details show up. When the slide is ready, it is put on the microscope's 'stage'–a platform with a hole in the middle–and held steady with clips.

Underneath the stage is a small mirror which can be tilted to catch the light, either from a window or from an electric lamp. The mirror turns the light rays and reflects them up through the hole in the stage and the slide that has

been placed over it. In an expensive microscope there are extra lenses called condensers between the mirror and the stage, and these focus the light and make it stronger.

After passing through the slide and

Right An optical microscope, showing condenser lenses which concentrate the light reflected by the mirror underneath the stage, and extra projector lenses near the top of the turret to give greater magnification. All the lenses between the object and the observer's eye must be correctly focused if the object is to be seen clearly.

If you're buying a microscope, the best advice is to spend as much as you can afford. It should be as heavy as possible so that it holds the slide steady. When the lenses are properly adjusted, they should let clear white light pass through them, without rainbow-coloured edges.

Below A section of a sponge seen through an optical microscope.

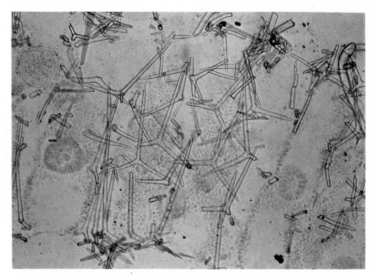

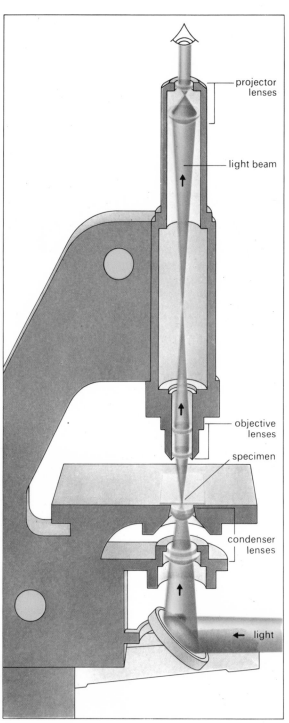

projector lenses

light beam

objective lenses

specimen

condenser lenses

← light

the object on it, the light rays go through the object lens, which focuses them. At the top of the tube of the microscope, which is called the 'turret', there may be more lenses, projector lenses, to focus and strengthen the image even more. Finally, the light rays reach the lens in the eyepiece and are seen by the viewer.

Using a microscope is not easy at first, but it is well worthwhile learning to do it properly. Slides must be prepared with great care with no finger-marks or dust on them. The slide must be adjusted on the stage so that the light will shine through the object. The mirror must be tilted at exactly the right angle to catch the light and throw it up through the lenses. Then the object must be brought into focus by adjusting the screw-knobs on the side of the turret. But the reward for all this care and effort is that the microscope will open your eyes to a whole new world.

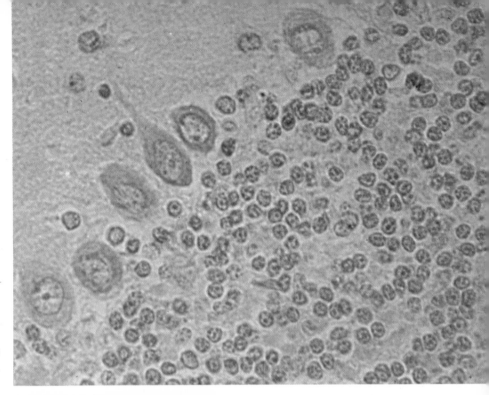

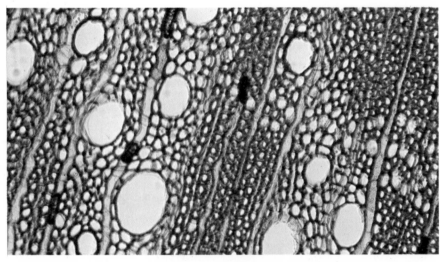

Above Cells of the European oak tree under an optical microscope. The sample has been stained to make it more easy to see.

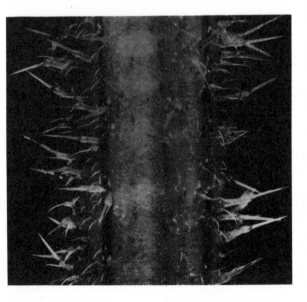

Right A section of the stem of a stinging-nettle, seen under an electron microscope. The pointed hairs contain the sting. They break off when they pierce the skin, releasing a small amount of acid which causes the rash and irritation.

Above These are the cells of a part of the human brain called the cerebellum. It was the invention of the microscope that led to the discovery that all living things, plant and animal, are made up of cells. The discovery was made by an English scientist, Robert Hooke, in 1665, when he was studying thin slices of cork under a microscope. There are about 1,000,000,000,000,000 cells in the human body.

The object to be examined under the microscope may be solid. As it will not let light pass through it, the usual arrangement of the mirror beneath the stage will not work. In this case a mirror is placed above the object, and light is shone down on to the stage.

Microscopes have been in use for nearly 400 years, but until photography was invented there was no way of storing the image or studying it away from the eyepiece. Now scientists can photograph the image in a microscope and study the result for as long as they like. When the photograph is developed, it can be enlarged so that the image is even more greatly magnified.

Looking at life under a microscope is fascinating, but of course it's much more than an interesting hobby. Microscopes have enabled doctors to find out more about diseases and how to cure them. A drop of your blood can be put under the microscope to see if it contains the right chemicals for growth and good health. The microscope is an 'extra eye' that helps us to know more about ourselves and our world—and also helps to keep us fit.

X-rays

We are able to see because our eyes can pick up light-waves coming from the things that we look at. We are able to hear because the vibrations set up by the object we are listening to travel along sound-waves to our ears. But there are other waves travelling through the air that human beings are not able to pick up. X-rays are among these. They are shorter than the waves of visible light and, like radio-waves, they can be picked up only with special machines.

When you look at your hand, you see only the outside layer—the skin, and the pink colour of the flesh underneath. If you had eyes that could see X-rays, you would be able to see the muscles and bones underneath the skin and flesh.

Then you would know what your hand is made of!

Of course, no human being has X-ray eyes. X-rays can pass through materials that normally stop light, just as ordinary light can pass through glass.

X-ray machines make X-rays and then 'shine' them on to the object being X-rayed. The result can either be seen straight away on a screen or be photographed for study later.

The main part of an X-ray machine is the tube. This is similar to the tube of a television set, and its job—as in a television set—is to produce a movement of electrons. But the electric current in an X-ray machine is very much higher than in any machine in your home.

The inside of the tube is a vacuum and contains two pieces of metal—a piece of wire called a cathode and a flat piece of metal called an anode. When the cathode is heated by passing electricity through it, streams of electrons—particles charged with negative electricity—are given off. These are free to move in the vacuum of the tube and they are drawn towards the anode, which has a positive electric charge. When they reach the anode, moving very fast, they suddenly slow down, almost to a stop. Their energy changes from movement to heat, but a small part of it becomes X-rays. These would escape from the tube in all directions unless they were prevented.

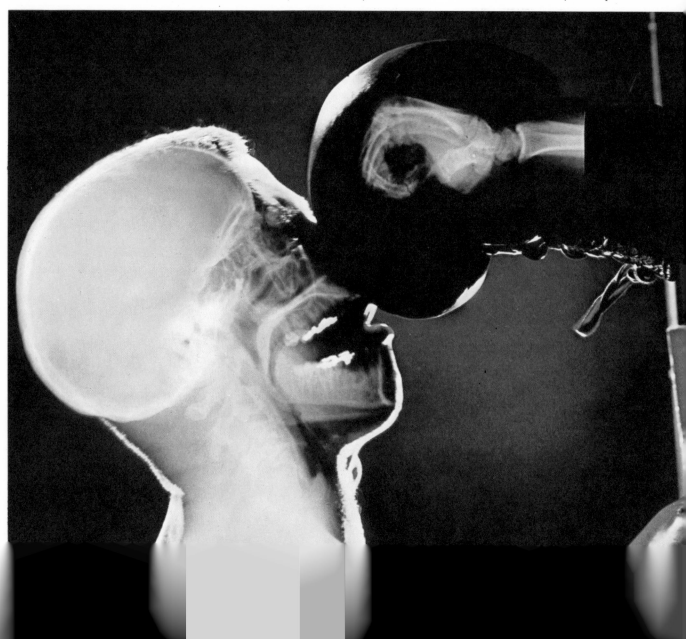

Thick lead is one of the things that even X-rays can't pass through, so it is used for the outer casing of the tube except in one place, where the X-rays can escape through glass. If they pass through an object, some of them are absorbed and others travel on. The screen of an X-ray machine is made of a substance sensitive to X-rays and it shows up the pattern made by the X-rays that reach it. Where the X-rays have difficulty in passing through—as they would if your hand were being X-rayed and they had to try to pass through the bones—the screen looks white.

X-rays can be dangerous. They can damage healthy living tissue and even affect the development of the bones in young children. For this reason people must not be exposed to them unnecessarily. Doctors who want to use X-rays to study their patients' illnesses take X-ray photographs. Photography with X-rays is called radiography. When an X-ray photograph is taken, the rays pass through the object only for a small fraction of a second—too short a time to do any harm.

X-ray photographs are used a great deal by doctors and dentists. They show up broken bones, decayed teeth and foreign objects that have entered the body such as coins or bullets. They also show parts of the body where a disease like cancer or tuberculosis has started. X-ray machines in vans are sent round to 'screen' large numbers of people for such diseases. X-ray photographs are taken, and when they have been developed they are checked for signs of disease. In this way many people's lives are saved because the disease is seen and treated before it becomes too serious.

Industry, too, uses X-rays. A bar of steel photographed by X-rays will reveal any hidden faults inside that may make it dangerous or difficult to use. X-rays are even used by dealers in old paintings, who can find out if a picture has been painted on top of an older one, as often happened when poor artists could not afford new canvas.

But why are they called X-rays? The answer takes us back to the German scientist Wilhelm Roentgen, who first discovered them. He found them by accident when he was doing an experiment with electrons in a glass tube. The X-rays given off made a glow on a chemically coated screen that happened to be in his laboratory. He didn't know what the rays were, so he called them X-rays because x in science stands for the unknown. And the name has stuck.

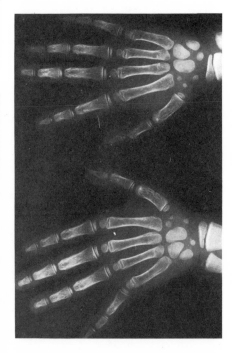

Above An X-ray of the hands of a four-year-old boy shows that the bones have not yet formed completely, especially at the wrist. If any of the bones had been damaged, this would have shown up clearly.
Left An X-ray photograph of a hand in a boxing-glove hitting a boxer's head. The picture was taken using film sensitive to colour and X-rays.
Right The Coolidge X-ray tube is used in most of today's X-ray machines. The stream of electrons from the cathode is shown by the blue arrow. X-rays (the red arrows) are given off when the electrons strike the anode. One problem with X-ray machines is that they give off tremendous heat which would quickly burn up the anode. To avoid this, in modern machines the anode rotates so that the electrons strike a different part. By the time the hot part of the anode comes round again it will have cooled.

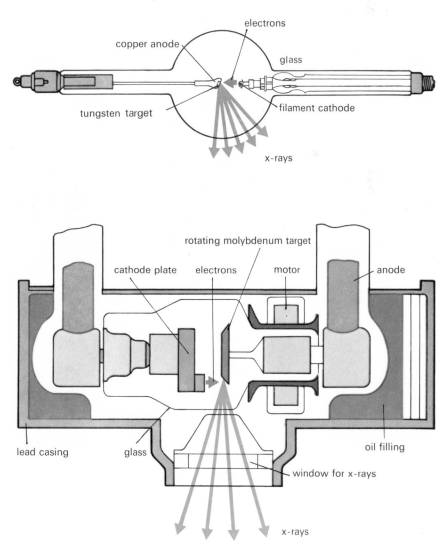

89

An oil-rig

When there is oil under the ground, it is not very difficult to drill down for it. But more and more of the world's oil supplies come from deposits under the sea.

Finding the oil is the job of the drilling-rig, a huge half-ship, half-building which is supported on legs reaching down to the sea-bed, with floats and anchors to keep it as steady as possible in the water. On the deck of the drilling-rig are a helicopter landing area, stores areas for the heavy equipment that will be used, living quarters for the crew and workshops for the engineers and drillers. In the centre of the rig is the drilling area, with a lattice-work tower called the 'derrick' over it.

Oil is found by drilling down into the earth and rock with a sharp-toothed cutting tool called a bit. The bit is connected to the drilling-machine—a diesel engine—by a 'string' of steel pipes, each 27 metres long. Up on the derrick men guide the lengths of pipe into place. Below on the drilling deck each new length of pipe is connected to the one before. The 'string' built up in this way may be as long as three kilometres or more.

When the bit on the end of the string reaches the sea-bed, it starts to drill a hole. Grinding away at the rock, the bit gets very hot and would soon wear out if it were not lubricated. A mixture of clay and water is pumped down the inside of the string and into the borehole under

pressure. The mud travels back up the borehole outside the string, bringing with it the shavings of drilled rock.

It can take several months to strike oil—or, of course, it may turn out that the drill is in the wrong place and there is no oil to be found. During all this time the workers on the rig work two weeks on and one off, returning to their homes for their week's leave. On the rig they have comfortable living quarters, excellent food and entertainments such as film shows. But the work is hard and often interrupted by storms and heavy seas, sometimes strong enough to cast the rig adrift or even capsize it. In rough seas drilling has to stop because the swaying of the rig might cause the string

Above This drilling-rig is at work off the coast of Texas, USA. As the coast is so near, this rig will be working in fairly shallow water. The five columns sticking up in front of the derrick are legs which can be lowered into the water to give it a firm base.

to break. The man whose job it is to keep the rig steady over the well being drilled is the marine superintendent—the 'captain' of the rig—who works in a control tower with instruments that record any movement.

On the sea-bed below is the well-head, a kind of seal which prevents oil from coming up too fast and spilling into the surrounding sea. There are television cameras at the well-head which keep watch on the drilling operation

and show it on screens up on the rig.

If oil is found, a sample is taken and checked to find out if it is of good quality. Meanwhile, geologists try to work out how much oil there is down below. They examine some of the drill shavings brought up and also take readings with an instrument called a 'gravimeter', which can show what kind of rocks are below.

If the sample proves satisfactory and the oil find is worth while, the men on the oil-rig check the well-head and then leave for another site. The rig is 'closed down', all the movable supplies and equipment are taken off by ship or helicopter, and the drilling crew flies home for some leave. Only a small skeleton crew is left on board. The supports and anchors are taken up, and tugs are sent out to tow the rig away.

Towing oil-rigs is a very tricky operation, because they are designed to stay steady and they don't move easily through the water. In the North Sea between England and western Europe towing is done only during the few summer months when the sea is at its calmest. These few months are called the 'weather window'.

The drilling-rig is replaced at the site of the find by a similar rig which is called a production platform. The job of the men on the production platform is to bring the oil ashore. This may be done by connecting a pipeline from the well-head across the sea-bed to an oil terminal on the nearest coast, or by piping the oil up to the platform and storing it until a tanker comes alongside to carry it away.

When it comes from the well, oil looks something like black treacle. At this stage it is called 'crude oil', and it is a mixture of many different kinds of substances. When it arrives ashore, it is sent to a refinery where, by being heated, the various different substances are separated. Light gases are boiled off first, followed by petrol. From then on the oil coming off gets gradually thicker. Paraffin and diesel oil are followed by heavier lubricating oils and grease. Only then are we able to use the oil products that started their journey several kilometres underneath the waves.

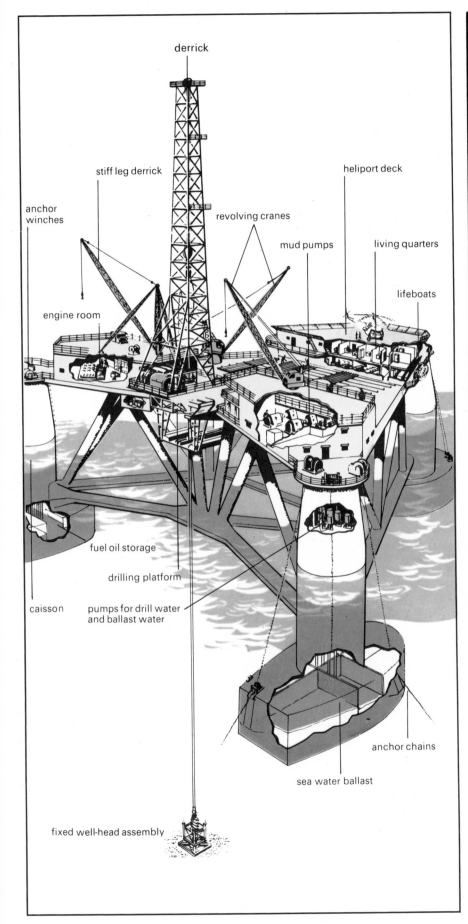

derrick

stiff leg derrick

anchor
winches

revolving cranes

mud pumps

heliport deck

living quarters

engine room

lifeboats

fuel oil storage

drilling platform

caisson

pumps for drill water
and ballast water

anchor chains

sea water ballast

fixed well-head assembly

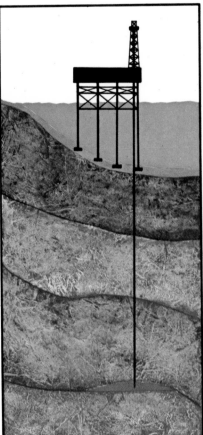

Above The legs of a drilling rig are adjustable so that it stands firmly in place, resting on the sea-bed. Pockets of oil–and of natural gas–lie buried hundreds of metres under the sea between layers of rock. Scientists find out where the oil is by drilling out and testing samples of rock. Oil-bearing rocks can be identified by experts from the types of fossils they contain. Sometimes, when oil is found, it is brought to the surface by the pressure of natural gas, but in other cases it must be pumped up to the rig.

Left When drilling for oil in the North Sea began about ten years ago, new kinds of rigs had to be designed and built. No one had ever drilled in such deep water before or in such a stormy sea. Tides and currents sweeping round the north of Scotland and up the English Channel make the North Sea especially rough and dangerous. The rig's three 'caissons' are floats which can be filled with sea-water to steady the rig in the water or used for storage. Heavy equipment can be landed on the rig from ships. Smaller supplies and the crew arrive by helicopter.

A power station

When man first arrived on the Earth, his only source of power was himself. He had to pull a plough, cut his own corn, make his own food, and so on. Gradually, he has discovered other sources of power—first animals like the horse and the ox, and then fuels such as wood and coal. A really big moment in man's story came when the steam-engine was invented, using wood or coal to heat water and then using the steam to drive machinery. Another big moment was the discovery that oil could be used as a source of power.

But while a fire can be made with wood or coal as fuel, not all sources of power can be used for every kind of purpose. You couldn't run your TV set on oil or gas! The most useful kind of power in our world is electric power, which can be made to do almost anything from lighting and heating our homes to driving machinery. Electricity can be made from almost any fuel.

In most of the world's power stations electricity is made by producing steam which drives a turbine. This is what is happening in the power station shown

in the diagrams. In this case the steam is made using coal as the fuel.

The coal is ground to dust, and air is added making a very explosive mixture which burns readily in the furnace. The fire heats the water in the steam tubes, and the steam flows at very high pressure through the steam drum into pipes where it is made even hotter. Then it is 'blown'—very hot and at high pressure—into a steam turbine.

A turbine is a shaft with blades sticking out from it. When the steam strikes the blades, it pushes them away and so makes the shaft turn in the same way as the sails of a toy windmill are made to turn when you blow on them.

The turbine shaft is connected to the

Below A coal-fired power station. 1 Conveyor belt. 2 Coal tipper. 3 Bunker. 4 Weigher. 5 Grinding mill. 6 Boiler house. 7 Fan. 8 Air heaters. 9 Hot-air ducts. 10 Furnace burners. 11 Main fan. 12 Furnace. 13 Cold water. 14 Steam drum. 15 Superheater. 16 Valve. 17 Steam turbine. 18 Re-heater. 19 Condenser. 20 Heaters. 21 'Economizer'. 22 Electrostatic precipitator. 23 Fan. 24 Flue. 25 Chimney.

coil of a generator which turns with it. A generator is a coil of wire inside a circular arrangement of magnets. As the coil turns, an electrical current flows through it, and this is the current that the power station sends out to its customers.

At present most power stations use either coal or oil as fuel, but because of fears that the world's supply of these will run out the search is on for other ways of making electricity. In countries with mountains and fast-flowing rivers—such as parts of Africa and North America—water-power is used. The water drives a water turbine, and this produces electricity in the same way as in a coal-fired power station. Another kind of fuel is nuclear fuel. This produces the energy to heat the water in the steam pipes. A further way of making electricity is by harnessing the sun's energy by means of solar cells. Unfortunately, very many such cells are needed, and so the process is expensive. It has been suggested that we should build windmills again—not, this time, to grind corn, but to turn the coil of a generator.

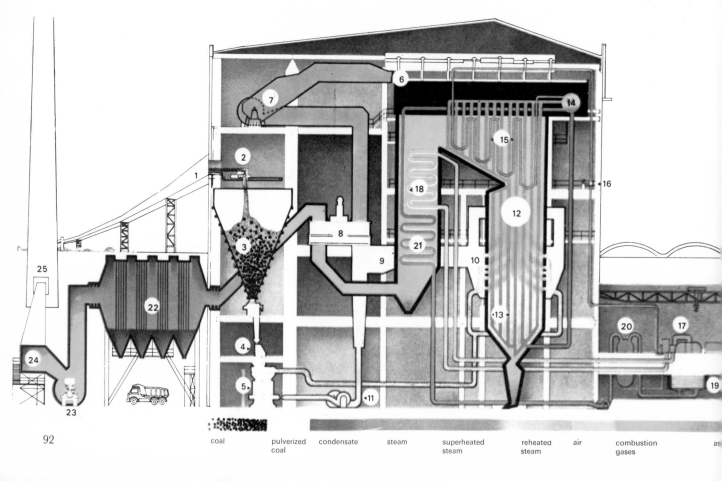

coal   pulverized coal   condensate   steam   superheated steam   reheated steam   air   combustion gases

But whatever source of energy a power station uses, it does the same job: it converts energy of another kind into electrical energy. Electricity has the great advantage that it can do nearly all the work that needs to be done in factories and farms and in our homes.

The electric current produced by a power station may have to travel a long way across country. The stronger a current, the farther it travels without losing power, so power station electricity is boosted for its journey to a very high voltage. It then travels along wires stretched high between pylons, safely out of the way of people and buildings. Before we can use it in our homes, it must be changed back into a low voltage suitable for our cookers, heaters, lights and so on. Any mains electricity is dangerous, however, so *never* try any experiments with it. If you need a source of electricity for your own experiments, use batteries.

Right A power station in southern France which collects the sun's energy and uses it to make electricity.
Below A diagram showing the processes carried on at the power station shown on the opposite page. Steam turns the blades of the turbine, and this turns the coil in the generator. From the generator electricity will flow out of the power station into the network of high tension lines that will carry it across country.

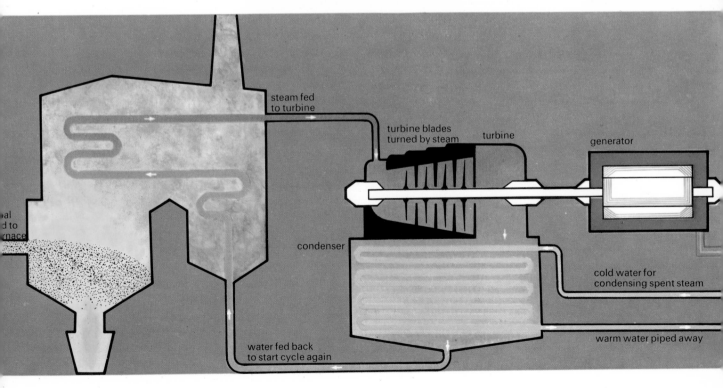

steam fed to turbine

turbine blades turned by steam

turbine

generator

al d to nace

condenser

cold water for condensing spent steam

water fed back to start cycle again

warm water piped away

Acknowledgments

The author and publisher would like to thank those who have given their permission for illustrations to be reproduced in this book. All diagrams are reproduced by permission of Orbis Publishing Limited.

Aldus Books 24–5 (NASA), 69 (Ken Cotton), 85t

Alfa Romeo 18t

Bavestrelli, Bevilacqua and Prato 86l

Beken of Cowes 42b

Boardman, Ron 87t, 87c

Bonetti, Terreni 59c

Brierley, Paul 34–5

British Rail Southern Region 65b

California Institute of Technology 33b

Camera Press 12l, 21b, 29b, 52t, 79 (J Pasan), 87b, 90 (Maurice and Sally Landre)

CIT 39bl

CNRS 93t

Colorific (Barbara Wace) 59b, 59t, 64l

Courtaulds Ltd 92

Daily Telegraph Colour Library 14–15

Favre 77t

Goodyear 11

Gregorio, A. de 62l

John Hillelson Agency 78 (Howard Sochurek), 88

Michael Holford Library 81c

IGDA 8t, 13bl, 13c, 19t, 20t, 21t, 29t, 33t, 48b, 70t, 74b 75b

Independent Television News Ltd 72, 73, 74t, 75t, 75c

Keystone 8b, 60–1, 81t

Leeds Royal Infirmary (89l (Dr Peacock)

Lick Observatory 39br

London Planetarium 40

Mansell Collection 10b

Mount Palomar 38br

Mount Wilson and Palomar Observatories 33c, 36t, 37b, 38–9

Museo Scuola di Cinematografia 38bl

NASA 12t, 26, 31br

Naval Photographic Center, USA, 44t

NSU Motorenwerke 56t

Photo Research 47

Picturepoint 13t, 32, 50t, 58t

Racaelli, Arch 23

Richner, B. 82

Rizzi, A. 62r, 84t

RM6 Melodium 68t

Rodriguez 43t

Seaphot 48 (Peter Scoones), 49

Spectrum 9

Studio T. di Tosi 30l

Time Life Books 66br (Albert Fenn)

Wyllie, Diana 28

Index

Figures in *italics* refer to
illustrations.

airlock 45
air-sea rescue 6
airship 10, *11*
Aldrin, 'Buzz' 28, *29*
Andromeda Spiral *38*
Apollo spacecraft *12*, 13, 23, 26, *27*,
   28, 29
Armstrong, Neil 28
Australia 53, 64
automobile 54–5

Baltimore and Ohio Railroad *52*, 53
Barton, Dr Otis 46
bat *20*
bathyscaphe 46
bathysphere 46
batteries, electric 53
Bell, Alexander Graham 66
Bell Sioux helicopter *8*
Bell X-1 aircraft 18
'bends', the 49
Bensen helicopter *8*
bevel gears *62*, 63
bicycle *63*
binary system 81
Buckingham Palace 8
buoyancy 44, *45*

California *33*, 46, 78
Cambridge, England 33, *34–5*
camera, photographic 36, 76–7
   television 74–5
Canadian Pacific Railroad 53
Cape Kennedy 22, *23*
cardinal points 82
Carlisle, England 50
channels, television 72
Chicago 52
Cockerell, Sir Christopher 42
colour television 72
communications satellite 30, 31
compass 82–3
compression 52
computer 41, 80–1
Concorde 19
Coolidge X-ray tube *89*
Crab nebula 33
crankshaft 54, *56*
crop-spraying 6
crude oil 90
Cygnus constellation 41

declination 82, 83
delta wings *18*, 19
developing, photographic 76, *77*
diesel–electric locomotive *52–3*
diesel engine 52–3, 90
Diesel, Rudolf 52–3
director, television 75
disc brakes 55
disc recording 70–1
diving-suit 49
double helical gears *63*
drilling-rig 90, *91*
drogue *12*, *13*
drum brakes *55*

dynamo 53

eclipse 40
Edison, Thomas Alva 70
Effelburg radiotelescope *35*
ejector seat 13
electron microscope 86, 87
elevator 64–5
English Channel 21, 42, 91
escalator 64–5
escape hatch 45
Europa airship 10. *11*
Evening Star locomotive *50*

fireworks 22–3
fish-eye lens 76, 77
flow chart *80*
'free fall' parachuting 13, *14–15*
frogmen 49

gallery, television studio 75
Garnerin, André *12*
gas, natural 91
gearbox 54, *58*
gears 62–3
Goodyear airship 10, *11*
gravimeter 90
gravity 6, 26
gyrocompass 83

Hale reflector *36*, 37
Heathrow Airport, London 8
helical gears *62*, 63
helicopter 6–8, 91
helium 10, 49
Hercules constellation *39*
herringbone gears *62*
hi-fi 68
Hindenburg airship 10
Hooke, Robert 87
hovercraft 42–3
hydrofoil 42–3
hydrogen 10, 22, 23
hydroplane 44–5

India 50
Indian Pacific Railway 53
infra-red rays 78
instant camera 77
ionosphere 69

jet engine 16–17, 78
Jodrell Bank radiotelescope *32*

kerosene 16, 22, 23, 25
Kodak company 77

Lakehurst, New Jersey 10
laser 84, *85*
lens 36–7, 40, 76, 86–7
Leonardo da Vinci 6, 12
life support system 26, *27*
live broadcasts 74
Liverpool, England 50
Lockheed Tri-Star aircraft 17
London 8, 40
London Planetarium 40
Los Angeles 8, 81
lubber line 83

Lunar Module 28
Lyre constellation 41

Mach 1 18–19, 80
magnetic north 82
Mars 28
Medicina, Italy, observatory *33*
memory bank 81
microscope 36, 86–7
MiG-21 fighter 17
Milky Way 40
Mirage fighter 17
missile warning system 21
moon rover 28
moonshoes 26, *27*
Moto-Cross *60–1*
motor car 54–5
motor cycle 58–9
Mount Palomar observatory *33*, *36*, 37,
   38–9

Newton, Isaac 36
New York 30
North Sea 90
nuclear fuel 92

oil-rig 90
optical microscope *86*, 87
orbit 30–1
Otis, Elisha G. 65
outboard motor 59
oxygen 22, 23, 25, 26, 46, 49

parachute 12–13, 30
periscope 45
perspex 8, *9*
petrol engine 54–5, 56, 58–9
phonograph *69*
photography 37
Piccard, Jacques 46
planetarium 40–1
planetary gears *63*
Pleiades *38–9*
Polaroid camera 77
Pole-Star 41
Post Office Tower, London *69*
power station 92–3
Prince Philip, Duke of Edinburgh 8
printed circuit 74
print-out *81*
production platform 90
Proton I satellite *30*
pulsars 33
Purisima, bathysphere 46, *47*

quasars 33, *38*

rack-and-pinion steering *55*
radar 20–1
radiation 26, 88–9
radio 68–9
radiography 89
radiotelescopes 32–3
railways 50–1, 53
ramjet 17
reflector 37
refractor 36
ribbon microphone *68*
rockets 22–4